FEED YOUR
Athlete

DK | Penguin Random House

Publisher: Mike Sanders
Associate Publisher: Billy Fields
Executive Acquisitions Editor: Lori Cates Hand
Production Editor: Jan Lynn
Cover and Book Design: XAB Design
Photographer: Tom Hirschfeld
Food Stylists/Chefs: Tom Hirschfeld, Anthony Armstrong
Indexer: Johnna Dinse
Layout: Ayanna Lacey
Proofreader: Cate Schwenk

First American Edition, 2015
Published in the United States by DK Publishing
6081 E. 82nd Street, Indianapolis, Indiana, 46250

Copyright © 2015 Dorling Kindersley Limited
A Penguin Random House Company
15 16 17 18   10 9 8 7 6 5 4 3 2
001–279035–June/2015

A catalog record for this book is available from the Library of Congress
ISBN: 978-1-46543-537-8

Note: This publication contains the opinions and ideas of its authors. It is
intended to provide helpful and informative material on the subject
matter covered. It is sold with the understanding that the authors and
publisher are not engaged in rendering professional services in the
book. If the reader requires personal assistance or advice, a competent
professional should be consulted. The authors and publisher specifically
disclaim any responsibility for any liability, loss, or risk, personal or
otherwise, which is incurred as a consequence, directly or indirectly, of
the use and application of any of the contents of this book.

DK books are available at special discounts when purchased in bulk for
sales promotions, premiums, fund-raising, or educational use. For
details, contact: DK Publishing Special Markets, 345 Hudson Street,
New York, NY 10014 or SpecialSales@dk.com.

Printed and bound in the United States by Courier Kendallville

A WORLD OF IDEAS:
SEE ALL THERE IS TO KNOW

www.dk.com

MICHAEL KIRTSOS, MS, RD, CSSD, LDN
and **JOSEPH EWING**, RD, LDN

FEED YOUR
Athlete

A COOKBOOK TO FUEL HIGH PERFORMANCE

150 easy-to-make, easy-to-eat, natural recipes for on-the-go athletes

Contents

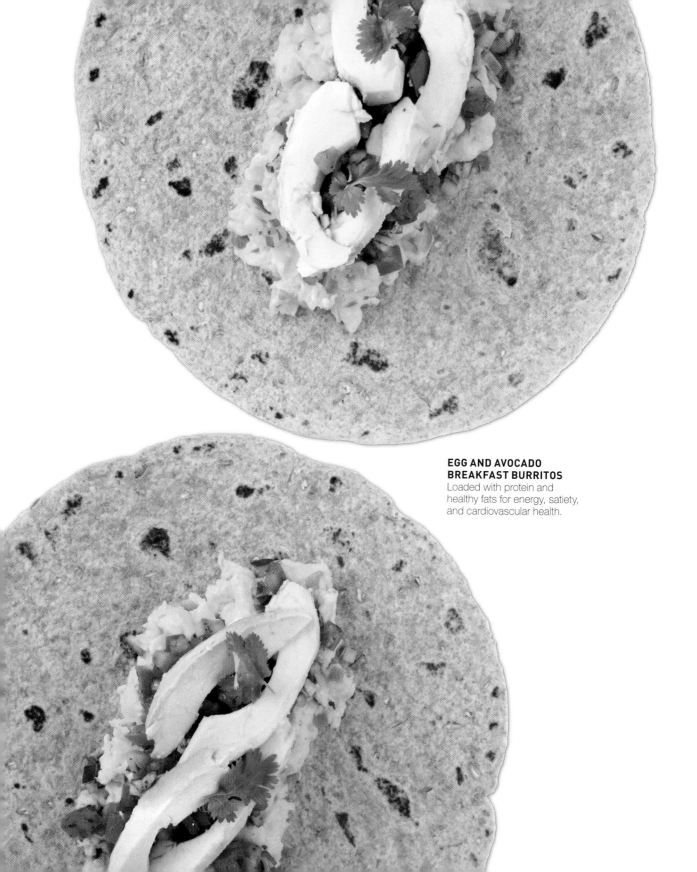

**EGG AND AVOCADO
BREAKFAST BURRITOS**
Loaded with protein and
healthy fats for energy, satiety,
and cardiovascular health.

Introduction

As an athlete, your body needs specific macro- and micronutrients to be a well-fueled, powerful, athletic machine. But how do you get all those nutrients in your diet, and when should you consume them in relation to your workout or athletic event? How many calories do you need, and how do you break down all this information into specific meals?

We designed *Feed Your Athlete* to be your one-stop nutrition manual and cookbook for the athlete in you and in your family. In these pages, you have access to a wealth of nutrition knowledge as well as more than 150 power-packed recipes and variations to fuel your body.

You learn the basics of nutrition, including macronutrients (carbohydrates, proteins, and fats) as well as various micronutrients (vitamins and minerals), and why they're important for the well-nourished athlete. You also explore fluids and electrolytes and the role they play in your performance on the field, in the gym, and more.

Are you a vegetarian or vegan athlete? Or do you have a gluten allergy or sensitivity? *Feed Your Athlete* features sections on feeding these specialized diets in addition to a number of delicious recipes adapted for these athletes.

Feed Your Athlete provides specific information on the nutritional needs of both endurance and strength athletes and helps you choose the best foods for the type of sports you participate in. We share tips and tricks on feeding a family of athletes, from real people with families full of athletes. We also help you stock your pantry, select essential cooking tools, and even give you hints on quick-cooking methods and meal assembly. We provide easy-to-follow information on making real-food portables and homemade sports drinks and smoothies, leaving out all the mystery ingredients from store-bought options.

What's more, *Feed Your Athlete* gives you 150 nourishing, whole-food meals and snacks for training, competition, and recovery for both endurance and strength athletes. Quick and easy preparation tips and nutritional information are also provided.

Further nutrition analysis has been done on each recipe to give you a comprehensive nutritional breakdown so you can accurately fit these foods into your dietary needs.

Feed Your Athlete makes it easy to fuel your body—and the bodies of your family of athletes—before, during, and after sporting events and training with all-natural, real-food recipes for meals, snacks, portables, sports drinks, and more that ensure peak performance.

ICONS
The recipes in this book feature icons that point out recipes geared for specific nutritional needs:

LOW FAT
Keeps calories down to avoid weight gain and promote cardiovascular health

HIGH PROTEIN
Gives fuel for strength and rebuilding muscle

HIGH CARB
Provides important fuel for endurance activities

HIGH FIBER
Is ideal for larger meals 3 to 5 hours before activity

LOW FIBER
Is best for digestion before competition and during recovery

How to Feed
Your Athlete

When you're training for a triathlon, another sporting event, or just working out at the gym, you need the right kind of fuel, in the right amounts, at the right times. In the following pages, we share what you need to know to feed your athlete—or yourself—the essential nutrients you need when you need them, as easily and deliciously as possible.

Curious about the difference between the needs for endurance and strength athletes? We explain the variances in this part. We also make it easy to understand the nutrition you need for the sports you do; delve into specialized dietary needs such as vegan, vegetarian, and gluten-free athletes; and teach you about vitamins and minerals—which ones are likely to be lacking in your diet and how to compensate. To make the "feeding" part easier, we help you stock your pantry with essential ingredients plus the tools you need to easily and efficiently prepare recipes. Finally, we give you quick-cooking and meal-assembly tips and pointers on preparing your own portables and sports drinks.

Being a nutritionally sound, well-fueled athlete has never been easier.

Nutrition **Basics**

Tailoring what you eat to your training schedule and the type of physical activity or sport you participate in can have a significant impact on how you perform. To perform at your best, you have to fuel your body the right way. In this section, we give you the basics for building a nutrition plan that works for you or the athletes you feed.

CARBOHYDRATES

Carbohydrates, or *carbs,* consist of sugars, starches, and fiber found in fruits, dairy products, grains, starchy vegetables (such as potatoes, sweet potatoes, corn, and peas), and beans.

Carbohydrate digestion begins in the mouth and takes place primarily in the small intestine. Broken-down carbohydrates are absorbed in the small intestine and transported to the liver, where glucose is stored as glycogen. When extra energy is needed, the liver can break down the stored glycogen to maintain normal blood glucose levels. Glucose may be used immediately for energy for a workout, or it can be stored as glycogen or fat.

Carbohydrates are the primary energy source for both strength and endurance athletes. Carbohydrates enable your body to use protein to build muscle instead of burning it for use as energy.

PROTEIN

Protein is found in beef, pork, chicken, turkey, fish, seafood, eggs, dairy products, nuts and nut butters, legumes, and grains.

Protein digestion takes place in the stomach and small intestine. Protein is eventually broken down into smaller amino acid molecules, which are absorbed in the small intestine and transported in the bloodstream. Once proteins are broken down into amino acids, they're used in the body as building blocks for the synthesis of hormones, neuro-transmitters, DNA (deoxyribonucleic acid), RNA (ribonucleic acid), enzymes, and the structural components of muscle. Your body can synthesize some amino acids on its own, but there are some amino acids your body can't synthesize and must obtain through food.

Protein is crucial for athletes; it provides the building blocks needed to build and repair muscle, which improves strength and power.

TUBERS
Potatoes are a great whole-food source of carbs. Sweet potatoes have the added benefit of extra fiber.

EGGS
Eggs are a rich and versatile source of protein that are quick and easy to cook.

FATS

Fats are found in various foods like oils, margarine or butter, nuts and nut butters, some fruits (such as avocados), dairy products, beef, pork, poultry, and fish.

Fat digestion begins in the mouth and takes place primarily in the stomach and small intestine. Fatty acids are absorbed in the small intestine, incorporated into lipoproteins and chylomicrons, and then transported in the bloodstream. Lipoproteins contain fats bound to proteins, which help the compound move through both the bloodstream and in and out of cells easier. Chylomicrons are part of a group of five lipoproteins (chylomicrons, very-low-density lipoprotein/VLDL, intermediate-density lipoprotein/IDL, low-density lipoprotein/LDL, and high-density lipoprotein/HDL) that contain triglycerides, phospholipids, cholesterol, and protein. These lipoproteins are used to transport dietary fats and cholesterol from the intestines to other areas in the body by way of the bloodstream.

Fatty acids not immediately used for energy production are stored as triglycerides in fat cells or inside muscle cells as intramuscular triglycerides. Through a process called lipolysis, the stored triglycerides are broken down into glycerol and three fatty-acid molecules and metabolized for energy.

Fats are a particularly important energy source for endurance athletes to preserve already-limited glycogen stores until they're needed while delaying fatigue and increasing exercise duration.

FISH
Fish are a good alternative to red meats as a protein source.

NUTS
Walnuts and other nuts pack a protein punch and help prevent dehydration after a workout.

VITAMINS AND MINERALS

Vitamins and minerals do not directly provide energy but are necessary for the body to conduct a number of metabolic processes, such as adequate growth and development, transportation of oxygen, and proper immune function.

Vitamins and minerals also serve as antioxidants, helping prevent free-radical damage in the body. Thiamin, riboflavin, niacin, vitamin B_6, vitamin C, zinc, folic acid, and vitamin B_{12} are just some vitamins that play key roles in a number of energy pathways in the body.

Vitamins and minerals act as cofactors that help protein molecules, such as enzymes, perform chemical reactions. Without adequate amounts of vitamins or minerals, several enzymes in the body would not be able to function.

Being deficient in one or several vitamins or minerals could affect your body's ability to produce energy and impair your athletic performance. Several factors can affect the amount of vitamins and minerals needed:

- Exercise intensity, duration, and frequency
- Temperature of the exercise environment
- Sweat and urine losses
- Gender
- Your nutritional status

Athletes participating in weight-category sports (such as gymnasts, dancers, boxers, weightlifters, and jockeys) are at the highest risk of inadequate vitamin and mineral intake due to their training intensity and low energy intake to maintain weight.

CITRUS
Citrus fruits such as tangerines are a good source of vitamin C and an easy portable snack.

FLUIDS AND ELECTROLYTES

Maintaining adequate fluid and electrolyte intake during physical activity is just as important as sufficient energy intake when it comes to athletic performance. Being slightly dehydrated (a 1 percent or less loss of body weight during physical activity) can negatively affect your body's ability to handle the stress of the activity and can impair performance.

Your body mainly loses fluids from sweat, urine output, feces, and breathing while losing electrolytes primarily via urine and sweat. Receptors in the hypothalamus and vascular system relay information back to the brain about the blood and the amount of water it contains. This information helps your body regulate hydration status by signaling when you need to consume more fluid or excreting excess fluid your body doesn't need.

Remember that thirst alone is not a good indicator of hydration status. The color of your urine, for example, can signal whether you're dehydrated. The darker the urine, the more hydration you need.

Minerals such as sodium, chloride, potassium, calcium, iron, and magnesium are key electrolytes in maintaining hydration status, and all can be lost via sweat. Your beverage intake during and after physical activity should include some carbohydrates in the form of glucose and sodium. Glucose provides an additional energy source during physical activity and helps promote glycogen synthesis after activity. Sodium helps retain fluid and makes you feel thirsty, which prevents dehydration during physical activity and promotes rehydration during recovery periods.

You also can replenish electrolytes by eating foods rich in sodium, chloride, potassium, calcium, iron, and magnesium. These are available in a wide variety of foods, including avocados, bananas, cantaloupe, oranges, raisins, figs, olives, tomatoes, broccoli, celery, leafy greens, potatoes, beans, nuts, seeds, fortified and whole grains, seafood, cheese, milk, yogurt, and vegetable juices.

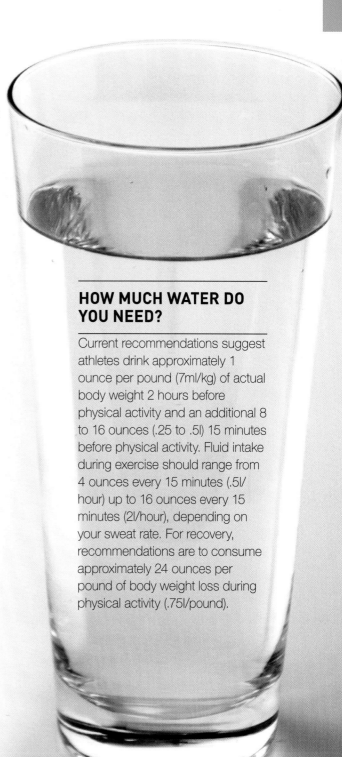

HOW MUCH WATER DO YOU NEED?

Current recommendations suggest athletes drink approximately 1 ounce per pound (7ml/kg) of actual body weight 2 hours before physical activity and an additional 8 to 16 ounces (.25 to .5l) 15 minutes before physical activity. Fluid intake during exercise should range from 4 ounces every 15 minutes (.5l/hour) up to 16 ounces every 15 minutes (2l/hour), depending on your sweat rate. For recovery, recommendations are to consume approximately 24 ounces per pound of body weight loss during physical activity (.75l/pound).

HOW YOUR BODY TURNS FOOD INTO FUEL

When you eat food, it goes through a series of chemical reactions inside your body, with the end products being carbon dioxide, water, heat, and energy in the form of adenosine triphosphate (ATP). The energy needed to perform physical activity is produced from the breakdown of chemical bonds found in carbohydrates, proteins, and fats, and the production of ATP.

Where Energy Comes From

The most energy is provided from the breakdown of carbohydrates and fats. Protein is rarely used as an energy source because the amino acids in protein are used for building and maintaining muscle, although the body can use protein as an energy source when carbohydrate intake is inadequate. The liver and muscles can store glucose as glycogen for later use as well as fat, in the form of intramuscular triglycerides, as an additional energy source.

Muscle cells also contain *phosphocreatine,* which provides energy during high-power, short-duration activities lasting a few seconds, such as sprinting, weightlifting, throwing, or a tennis serve. Muscle cells store only a small amount of phosphocreatine but can replenish ATP very quickly by donating phosphorus molecules to form new ATP molecules. Although this does not generate a large amount of ATP, it serves as an additional energy system to supply small amounts of ATP very quickly to muscle cells when the demand for energy is very high. Creatine is found in meats—especially wild game like venison, elk, bison and buffalo, free-range turkey, chicken, lamb, and veal—and wild-caught fish.

The Process of Glycolysis

As ATP is consumed, the by-products of this reaction begin to build up and trigger another energy system, *glycolysis,* to increase its ATP production. Glycolysis is an energy system that can only use glucose or glycogen for energy production. It can occur with or without the presence of oxygen.

Without adequate oxygen present, glycolysis typically lasts for 1 to 3 minutes. If the physical activity continues at a high intensity past that point, hydrogen ions, one of the by-products of glycolysis, start to accumulate and contribute to the formation of a molecule called lactate. Lactate is metabolized by skeletal and heart muscle to provide energy.

Muscle Soreness

When levels of lactate begin to rise faster than the body can keep up with metabolizing it, the result is an accumulation of hydrogen ions, causing a decrease in the body's pH, making it a more acidic environment. This inhibits your body's ability to use fat for energy, which forces it to rely primarily on carbohydrates for energy. These factors are typically associated with muscle pain, soreness, and fatigue athletes may experience, which can decrease athletic performance.

Through adequate training and proper nutrition, your body can become more efficient at metabolizing lactate, which might help minimize the negative effects due to elevated lactate levels.

How ATP Translates to Performance

With adequate oxygen present, glycolysis produces ATP. Complete metabolism of 1 glucose molecule can produce 38 ATP molecules. This provides about 266 kilocalories (kcals) of available energy, or enough energy for a person who weighs 180 pounds (81.5kg) to run at 4 miles per hour (6km/hour) for 30 minutes.

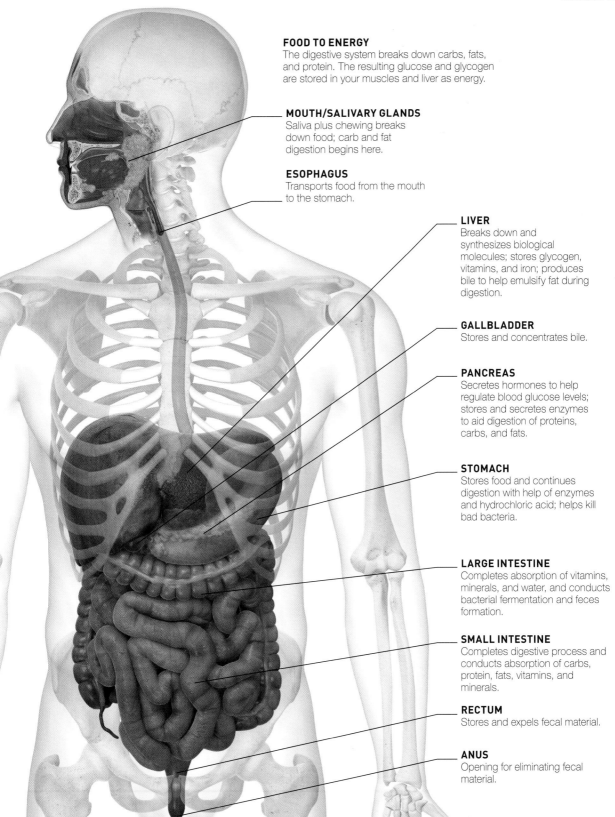

FOOD TO ENERGY
The digestive system breaks down carbs, fats, and protein. The resulting glucose and glycogen are stored in your muscles and liver as energy.

MOUTH/SALIVARY GLANDS
Saliva plus chewing breaks down food; carb and fat digestion begins here.

ESOPHAGUS
Transports food from the mouth to the stomach.

LIVER
Breaks down and synthesizes biological molecules; stores glycogen, vitamins, and iron; produces bile to help emulsify fat during digestion.

GALLBLADDER
Stores and concentrates bile.

PANCREAS
Secretes hormones to help regulate blood glucose levels; stores and secretes enzymes to aid digestion of proteins, carbs, and fats.

STOMACH
Stores food and continues digestion with help of enzymes and hydrochloric acid; helps kill bad bacteria.

LARGE INTESTINE
Completes absorption of vitamins, minerals, and water, and conducts bacterial fermentation and feces formation.

SMALL INTESTINE
Completes digestive process and conducts absorption of carbs, protein, fats, vitamins, and minerals.

RECTUM
Stores and expels fecal material.

ANUS
Opening for eliminating fecal material.

Determining Your Caloric and **Nutrient Needs**

Proper nutrition is essential to meet the energy demands of training and competition while maximizing performance. Inadequate nutrition can limit training gains, which impairs performance and overall health. Three factors are used together to determine nutritional needs: basal energy expenditure, energy balance, and body composition.

BASAL ENERGY EXPENDITURE

Basal energy expenditure (BEE) is the amount of energy your body uses to carry out fundamental metabolic functions such as breathing, kidney function, and blood circulation in a resting state. Genetics, age, gender, weight, lean body mass, and fat mass all can affect basal energy expenditure.

Women typically have more body fat and less muscle mass than men. Because fat is less metabolically active than muscle, this results in a lower basal energy expenditure for women.

Basal energy expenditure makes up 60 to 75 percent of daily energy needs and typically declines as you age due to loss of muscle mass. Another 10 percent of daily energy is spent on digesting and metabolizing food, which is called the thermic effect of food.

GREEN SALAD
A salad with greens and a vinaigrette dressing is a low-calorie way to get important nutrients.

ENERGY BALANCE

Consuming more calories than your total daily energy expenditure results in weight gain, typically in the form of fat. One pound (.5kg) of fat is equivalent to 3,500 calories. Eating fewer calories and exercising or burning more calories can result in safe weight loss. Consuming 500 fewer calories a day equals 3,500 calories a week, enough to lose 1 pound (.5kg) of fat. Burn an additional 500 calories a day through exercise, and you could lose 2 pounds (1kg) a week safely.

DAILY ENERGY EXPENDITURE (calories burned per day)

The following chart shows how your total amount of energy is spent in a typical day. Physical activity is the area you have the most control over and can manipulate.

THERMIC EFFECT OF FOOD
(digestion, absorption, and metabloism of energy): **10%**

BASAL ENERGY EXPENDITURE
(breathing, circulation, kidney function, etc.): **60 TO 70%**

PHYSICAL ACTIVITY: 20 TO 30%

CALCULATING YOUR CALORIE NEEDS

Several mathematic equations are used to estimate calorie needs, and you can find calculators online. The following table offers easy equations to determine your calorie needs using the calories-per-kilogram* method.

Goal	Equation
Weight loss	Weight in kg × 25
Weight maintenance	Weight in kg × 30
Weight gain	Weight in kg × 35

*1 kilogram is equal to 2.2 pounds. To determine your weight in kilograms, divide your weight in pounds by 2.2.

BODY COMPOSITION

Body composition is more than how much you weigh; it's a reflection of the body fat and muscle mass that combine to make up your weight. Several tools are available to assess body composition:

BMI   A relationship between body weight and height, body mass index (BMI) does not distinguish between muscle mass and fat mass. One way to calculate BMI is to divide your weight in kilograms by your height in meters squared. Or divide your weight in pounds by your height in inches squared and then multiply by 705.

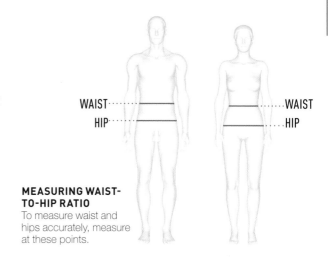

MEASURING WAIST-TO-HIP RATIO
To measure waist and hips accurately, measure at these points.

BMI CLASSIFICATIONS

There are six categories within BMI classifications, ranging from underweight to morbidly obese.

Classification	BMI Number
Underweight	less than 18.5
Normal weight	18.5 to 24.9
Overweight	25 to 29.9
Class I obesity	30 to 34.9
Class II obesity	35 to 39.9
Morbidly obese	more than 40

Waist-to-hip ratio   This method takes into account fat distribution. Where on the body a person carries excess fat can be a predictor for disease risk. Excess abdominal fat, for example, has been linked to increased risk of developing diseases like hypertension, hypercholesterolemia, cardiovascular disease, diabetes, stroke, osteoarthritis, sleep apnea, and gallbladder disease.

To calculate waist-to-hip ratio, divide your waist circumference in inches (or centimeters) by your hip circumference in inches (or centimeters). A waist-to-hip ratio close to .9 or higher for men and .8 or higher for women is associated with increased disease risk.

Waist circumference is also highly associated with disease risk. Waist circumference measurements above 40 inches (101.5cm) for men and above 35 inches (89cm) for women are associated with increased disease risk.

Overall body composition can affect physical activity and athletic performance. Carrying excess body fat requires more energy to move the excess weight. Expending these extra calories can decrease aerobic or endurance athletic performance. Excess body fat does not produce force like muscle does, resulting in less force production yet more weight to move, which requires more energy and can decrease overall speed, particularly in sports requiring speed and force production like sprinting, wrestling, boxing, skating, rowing, and gymnastics.

BODY FAT PERCENTAGES

Athletes carry 10 to 18 percent less fat than the average person and should not go below the essential fat levels.

	Men	Women
Essential fat	5%	12%
Athletes	5 to 14%	12 to 23%
Acceptable	15 to 20%	24 to 30%
Overweight	21 to 24%	31 to 36%
Obese	25% or greater	37% or greater

Eating for **Each Stage of Training**

The stage of training or the part of the sport season you're currently in can affect your nutrition needs. Many athletes break up a sport season into three phases: preparation, competition, and transition. Tailoring how you eat to where you are in your training can help to further improve your performance because the goal of each stage of training may be different, which may require different nutrients.

In-season carb loading focuses on increasing glycogen stores beyond normal capacity as a fuel reserve for endurance activity. It may only be beneficial for athletes who participate in continuous, intense endurance activity lasting 90 minutes or longer. Typically, athletes decrease training 6 days before an event, eating a normal mixed diet during the first 3 days consisting of at least 5 grams of carbs per kilogram (kg) of body weight followed by a high-carb diet for the last 3 days consisting of at least 10 grams of carbs per kg of body weight.

Adequate in-game carb intake is also crucial for performance. Consume easily digested low-fiber carbs with little to no fat and protein. During recovery, you have a small window to rebuild glycogen stores. Focus on low-fiber, low-fat, and moderate-protein foods.

NUTRIENT NEEDS FOR EACH STAGE OF TRAINING

Carb and protein needs increase during preparation and competition phases, whereas fat needs remain the same throughout.

Phase	Carbs Grams per kg Body Weight	Maximum Grams per kg Body Weight	Fat Grams per kg Body Weight
Preparation	5 to 12	1.2 to 1.7	0.8 to 1.0
Competition	7 to 12	1.4 to 2.0	0.8 to 1.0
Transition	4 to 7	1.2 to 1.4	0.8 to 1.0

THE PREPARATION PHASE

Your goal during this phase might be to increase the intensity of your sport-specific training and increase your resistance training to build new muscle, improve strength and power, and build up anaerobic conditioning.

Nutrition goals during this period include adequate carbohydrate and protein intake for building new muscle and repairing damaged muscle from physical activity. If your overall calorie intake is inadequate to meet your needs, your body will break down protein to provide energy and deplete muscle and liver glycogen stores, which can impair performance. If your overall calorie needs are met, protein can be used for building new muscle tissue and not for energy production.

PREPARATION PHASE NUTRIENT FOCUS

The following nutrients are essential for building endurance and intensity.

High carbs	Fluids
High protein	Vitamins and minerals

POWER-PACKED CAULIFLOWER TACOS
This portable, high-protein, high-carbohydrate dish is excellent for training days.

THE COMPETITION PHASE

Your competition phase goals should be to maintain strength, power, and conditioning gains while continuing to improve performance. Resistance training may decrease during this phase with a focus on increasing exercise intensity while decreasing volume, adding core-strengthening activities, and focusing on injury prevention. Additional training like plyometrics to improve speed, power, agility, and flexibility may be beneficial.

Your nutrition goals should focus on getting adequate carbs, protein, fluids, and vitamins/minerals, and limiting high-fiber foods immediately before competition and during recovery. High-fiber foods take longer to digest and may cause GI complications and delay glycogen synthesis.

THE TRANSITION PHASE

After the season is over, athletes typically go through a period of rest to allow their bodies to heal physically as well as psychologically from the demands of the preparation and competition phases.

Recreational-type physical activity may be beneficial during this period, such as swimming, jogging, volleyball, racquetball, and basketball. The focus of this physical activity should be on lower intensities and decreased volume.

Nutrition needs decrease at this time, as should intake. Decrease your carbohydrate, protein, and fat intake to offset your decreased physical activity. Focus on minimizing unintentional weight gain by limiting your intake of excess fat and carbohydrates, decreasing portion sizes, and eliminating additional snacking.

COMPETITION PHASE NUTRIENT FOCUS

Continue to get adequate carbs, protein, fluids, and vitamins and minerals, but limit fiber intake.

High carbs	Vitamins and minerals
High protein	Low fiber
Fluids	

TRANSITION PHASE NUTRIENT FOCUS

Reduce your intake of carbs and fat to avoid gaining weight due to decreased activity.

High protein	Low fat
Fluids	Low carb
Vitamins and minerals	

The Vegan or **Vegetarian Athlete**

Vegan and vegetarian athletes have to work harder to meet overall calorie needs because plant-based diets are lower in energy density and calories. The vegetarian diet meets carbohydrate needs more easily; however, it can be high in fiber. Focus on low-fiber foods immediately before, during, and immediately after activity to minimize GI complications and promote glycogen synthesis.

In general, vegetarian diets are typically high in carbohydrates and low in fat. Fat is also important because it makes up a part of all cell membranes, assists with the absorption of fat-soluble vitamins, and helps protect organs from injury.

Focus on foods high in mono- and polyunsaturated fats like avocados; olive, canola, sunflower, or safflower oil; and nuts and nut butters derived from peanuts, almonds, and cashews.

VEGETARIAN/VEGAN NUTRIENT RECOMMENDATIONS

Plant-based athletes need to ensure adequate carbohydrate, fat, and protein intake.

Nutrient	Recommended Intake
Carbohydrates	6 to 10g per kg
Fats	20 to 30% of calorie intake
Protein	1.3 to 1.8g per kg

PRIORITIZING FAT AND PROTEIN SOURCES

Vegan diets typically contain slightly less protein than general vegetarian diets because of the omission of animal products. Vegans and vegetarians may consume inadequate fat, so incorporate foods high in mono, and polyunsaturated fats to help meet energy and nutrient demands.

Protein needs vary depending on the type of physical activity and training required. Vegetarian athletes can meet these needs by increasing intake of plant-based protein foods like nuts, seeds, soy, veggie burgers, legumes, beans, and whole grains.

TOP 5 VITAMINS AND MINERALS FOR VEGAN AND VEGETARIAN ATHLETES

Vegan and vegetarian athletes need to consume enough of particular nutrients to avoid negative impacts on performance and possible nutrient deficiencies. Following is a list of the top vitamins and minerals essential for vegetarian athletes.

Vitamin B_{12}   Vitamin B_{12} is necessary for red blood cell formation, neurological function, and DNA synthesis, and is typically found in animal foods. Vegetarian athletes who consume eggs and dairy products will likely meet their B_{12} requirements. Vegan athletes need to ensure adequate intake of B_{12}-fortified foods, take a B_{12}-containing multivitamin, or supplement B_{12} individually. Risks of inadequate B_{12} intake include long-term damage due to neuropathy and anemia. Fortified breakfast cereals and grains, soymilk, and nutritional yeast products are good sources of B_{12}.

Calcium and vitamin D   Inadequate calcium and vitamin D intake is associated with increased risk of stress fractures and decreased bone density. Weight-bearing physical activity helps strengthen bones. General recommendations for calcium and vitamin D range from 1,000 to 1,200 milligrams a day for calcium and 5 to 15 micrograms a day for vitamin D, depending on your age.

High-calcium plant-based foods include fortified orange juice, fortified cereals, almonds and almond butter, green leafy vegetables like collard or turnip greens, broccoli, and brussels sprouts. Dairy products (for vegetarians) or fortified milk alternatives like soy, rice, or almond milk are also options.

Iron Most athletes are at increased risk for iron deficiency anemia due to inadequate intake of high-iron foods, iron losses via sweating, reduced absorption of iron, gastrointestinal bleeding, and (for women) menstrual blood loss. Iron is responsible for transporting oxygen in the body; without enough, athletic performance can be negatively affected. Animal sources of iron (heme sources) are absorbed better than vegetarian (nonheme sources). Iron absorption can be inhibited by compounds in certain foods such as polyphenols in cocoa and coffee; oxalates in tea, kale, beets, and chocolate; phytates in bran, nuts, seeds, and cereals; and eggs. Some compounds can enhance the absorption of nonheme iron, specifically vitamin C.

Good sources of iron include fortified breakfast cereals, dark green leafy vegetables such as kale and spinach, beans, tofu and soy beans, enriched breads, rice and pasta, potatoes and sweet potatoes, pumpkin seeds, quinoa, almonds, dried fruits, raisins, blackstrap molasses, tomato paste, peanut butter, and eggs (for vegetarians).

Zinc Zinc plays a role in several biochemical reactions and helps with proper function of the immune system. Zinc, like iron, is not absorbed as well due to higher concentrations of phytates. Vegetarian sources of zinc include hard cheeses, wheat germ, Swiss chard, kidney beans, chickpeas, lima beans, and pumpkin seeds.

Omega-3 fatty acids These essential fatty acids can't be synthesized by the body, so they must be obtained through dietary sources. Fish is typically a high source of omega-3s. Veg sources of omega-3s include flaxseed and flaxseed oil, chia seeds, raw walnuts, soybeans, winter squash, cauliflower, broccoli, blueberries, wild rice, mangoes, honeydew melon, and some leafy green vegetables. (Flaxseeds must be ground just before use to release the omega-3 fatty acids.)

Omega-3 fatty acids have many benefits, including reducing the risk of cardiovascular disease and helping decrease inflammation, which many athletes suffer from after physical activity or injury.

PLANT-BASED PROTEIN
Vegan and vegetarian athletes need to focus on foods high in protein and vitamins and minerals while monitoring fiber intake.

Nutrition for **Endurance Athletes**

The two most important nutrients for endurance athletes are carbohydrates, to improve performance, and protein, to help boost immunity. It's also important to get proper hydration before, during, and after exercise.

WHAT CARBS SHOULD YOU EAT WHEN?

Your body metabolizes different types of carbohydrates at various rates. Glucose is metabolized quickly, whereas fructose and galactose are not metabolized as fast because they must be transported to the liver first and then converted into glucose.

Typically, it's better to eat high-fiber foods for your larger meal 3 to 5 hours before physical activity. Low-fiber and low-fat foods are recommended immediately prior to, during, and after activity because fiber and fat can decrease rates of gastric emptying; cause GI complications like nausea, vomiting, diarrhea, or constipation; and may limit glycogen synthesis during recovery.

The following recommendations for carbohydrate intake for endurance athletes are based on studies by Louise Burke, department head of sports nutrition at the Australian Institute of Sport.

TIMING YOUR CARB INTAKE

Carbohydrate intake in the days leading up to a competition helps replenish your muscle glycogen stores. Carbohydrate intake 1 or 2 hours before a competition mainly helps replenish your liver glycogen stores and has little effect on your muscle glycogen stores.

A study by William Sherman, PhD, professor of sport science and wellness education at the University of Akron, recommends the following guidelines for carbohydrate intake during activity, based on body weight and the amount of time before the exercise and the duration of the exercise.

CARBOHYDRATE NEEDS FOR ENDURANCE ATHLETES

The amount of carbohydrates needed depends on activity level and body weight.

Situation	Daily Needs
Normal endurance sports	7 to 10g per kg body weight
Ultra-endurance sports	11g per kg body weight
Off season	5 to 7g per kg body weight

CARBOHYDRATE INTAKE GUIDELINES

Use the following charts to determine the correct amounts and timing of carb intake before and during activity.

CARBOHYDRATE INTAKE PRIOR TO ACTIVITY

Hours Before Exercise	Recommended Carb Intake
1	1g per kg body weight
2	2g per kg body weight
3	3g per kg body weight
4	4g per kg body weight

CARBOHYDRATE INTAKE DURING ACTIVITY

Hours During Exercise	Recommended Carb Intake
For each hour of activity	30 to 60g per kg body weight

Focus on low-fiber, low-fat, and high-carbohydrate foods. Look for the recipes in this book with these icons:

 **LOW FIBER**

 **LOW FAT**

 **HIGH CARB**

GREEK PASTA SALAD
This salad offers 42 grams carbs, 11 grams protein, and 13 grams fat.

DURING AND AFTER ACTIVITY

To improve your performance, you should consume some carbohydrate during physical activity that lasts 1 hour or longer. Carbohydrate intake during activity may provide an immediate fuel source, sparing liver and muscle glycogen until it's absolutely necessary. Edward Coyle, professor of exercise science at University of Texas at Austin, recommends consuming about 30 to 70 grams carbohydrate per hour of physical activity lasting 1 hour or longer.

Carbohydrate intake is needed within 30 to 60 minutes during the recovery phase after physical activity. During this phase, the enzyme that stimulates glycogen synthesis is elevated along with increased insulin sensitivity, both of which help promote rebuilding of glycogen stores. Research by John Ivy, PhD, chair of kinesiology and health education at University of Texas at Austin, found that consuming carbohydrate 2 hours or later after physical activity can reduce glycogen synthesis as much as 40 to 50 percent compared to the amount of glycogen that could be stored when consuming carbohydrate immediately after physical activity.

From this research, Ivy recommends the following for carbohydrate intake after exercise. (Adding some protein may help stimulate muscle protein synthesis and muscle glycogen synthesis.)

CARBOHYDRATE INTAKE AFTER EXERCISE

Consume carbs within 30 to 60 minutes immediately after exercise to aid in recovery, and eat more 2 hours later.

Timing	Recommended Carb Intake
Immediately afterward	1.5g per kg body weight
2 hours later	Additional 1.5g per kg body weight

AVOIDING REBOUND HYPOGLYCEMIA

Carbohydrate intake prior to exercise causes a rise in your blood glucose, which stimulates an insulin response to help return your blood glucose levels to normal. Physical activity stimulates the uptake of glucose from your bloodstream into your muscles to provide energy. The combination of these events can cause *rebound hypoglycemia,* or a delayed drop in blood glucose levels. Symptoms of hypoglycemia include dizziness, nausea, cold sweat, decreased ability to concentrate, loss of motor skill, and excessive hunger.

A 2003 study by Moseley and colleagues found that carbohydrate intake 5 to 15 minutes prior to physical activity instead of 45 to 60 minutes before should be adequate to minimize rebound hypoglycemia.

CARBOHYDRATE LOADING

Endurance performance is directly associated with muscle glycogen stores. Carbohydrate loading can improve endurance capacity by as much as 20 percent, according to some studies. Once muscle glycogen stores are depleted, endurance performance begins to decline. Through carbohydrate loading, however, you can build up muscle glycogen stores, giving you more time to participate in physical activity and improve your performance.

Carbohydrate loading is only beneficial if you're participating in continuous, high-intensity physical activity lasting 90 minutes or longer. It's not beneficial for shorter bouts of activity, like a 5K or 10K run or a short, high-intensity exercise like sprinting. Also, for carbohydrate loading to work, you must already be endurance trained.

Carbohydrate loading may be associated with muscle stiffness or feelings of heaviness due to increased water storage, but these symptoms should improve when the physical activity begins. This extra water retention can also lead to unintentional weight gain and may not be desired during weight-bearing physical activity.

Some complications of carbohydrate loading include hypoglycemia, challenges with meal preparation, gastrointestinal problems, increased injury risk, lethargy, irritability, and a decreased training level you might not be accustomed to.

Jonas Bergstrom and William Sherman have conducted multiple studies on carbohydrate loading and have developed the following guidelines. Method 1 is the most commonly used carb-loading schedule. Method 2, however, seems to be tolerated better, and with fewer complications, with similar results in terms of glycogen stores.

CARB-LOADING SCHEDULE, METHOD 1

Method 1 includes normal training; low-carb, high-protein, and high-fat meals for days 2 through 4; followed by rest and high-carb meals for days 5 through 7.

Day	Training	Diet
1	Glycogen-depleting exercise	Normal
2	Normal training	Low carb, high protein, high fat
3	Normal training	Low carb, high protein, high fat
4	Normal training	Low carb, high protein, high fat
5	Rest	High carb
6	Rest	High carb
7	Rest	High carb

TAGLIATELLE
Pasta is a well-known source
of carbs and a traditional
carb-loading choice for athletes.

CARB-LOADING SCHEDULE, METHOD 2

Method 2 features gradually declining exercise intensity, with a high-carb
diet for the final 3 days.

Day	Training	Diet
1	Glycogen-depleting exercise	Normal
2	Normal training	Normal
3	Training at half intensity	Normal
4	Training at half intensity	Normal
5	Training at quarter intensity	High carb
6	Training at quarter intensity	High carb
7	Rest	High carb

THE POWER OF PROTEIN FOR ENDURANCE

Protein needs increase for endurance athletes due to the high training volumes and long duration of physical activity, which speed the rate of protein metabolism. Protein needs also increase because your body has to increase the capillary density of your muscles used for endurance activity, make more mitochondria for energy production, and increase the number of enzymes needed to produce ATP.

PROTEIN RECOMMENDATIONS

Position paper statements endorsed by the Academy of Nutrition and Dietetics and the American College of Sports Medicine recommend a range from 1.2 to 1.4 grams per kilogram of actual body weight per day for endurance athletes. Protein metabolism can range anywhere from 2 to 6 percent of total energy expenditure for endurance physical activity. As carbohydrate stores begin to run low during prolonged endurance activity, the energy supplied from amino acid metabolism may increase up to 10 percent of total energy expenditure. Once protein is broken down, all amino acids can be used for energy, but six amino acids are metabolized within the muscle cell.

PROTEIN INTAKE FOR ENDURANCE ATHLETES

The top sports medicine associations recommend the following protein intake guidelines.

| Minimum | 1.2g per kg body weight per day |
| Maximum | 1.4g per kg body weight per day |

Look for recipes in this book with this icon, which signals a good source of protein:

HIGH PROTEIN

HAZELNUTS
Nuts are a convenient and portable source of protein to take along to endurance events.

BRANCHED-CHAIN AMINO ACIDS
Three of the amino acids metabolized in the cell are called isoleucine, leucine, and valine, or branched-chain amino acids. These can be used for energy in the muscle as muscle glycogen stores begin to run low. Research is currently being done on branched-chain amino acids and their potential benefit to improving athletic performance, delaying fatigue, and improving immune function.

IMMUNITY ISSUES FOR ENDURANCE ATHLETES

During endurance exercise, you have an increased exposure to airborne bacteria and viruses due to an increased rate of breathing and how much air you inhale. This, combined with psychological stress, poor nutrition, and extreme temperatures, might contribute to depressed immune function and increases the risk of developing an infection, typically in the form of upper respiratory tract infections.

During recovery, consuming carbohydrates with some protein might help stimulate muscle glycogen store replenishment, possibly due to insulin stimulation and secretion. Protein intake contributes to insulin secretion, similar to carbohydrate intake. Protein intake during recovery might also be beneficial in helping repair muscle proteins that have been damaged and aid in the production of immune cells to help protect against bacterial and viral infections.

HYDRATION IS KEY

Endurance athletes have increased fluid needs due to fluid losses from sweating and water vapor lost when breathing. Through training, endurance athletes can improve their body temperature regulation by maintaining a lower core body temperature, increased blood volume and skin blood flow, increased size of sweat glands, and an earlier onset of sweating.

As you participate in physical activity, your body temperature increases and you begin to sweat. As sweat evaporates, it helps reduce your body temperature. A dehydrated state, when your body temperature increases above normal, can result in increased release of epinephrine, norepinephrine, and free radicals. These compounds begin to deplete glycogen stores and can cause fatigue, heat exhaustion, or heat stroke, particularly in a hot and humid environment.

FLUID REPLACEMENT

Current recommendations for fluid replacement for athletes before, during, and after athletic activity, as shown in the following table, are based on timing and water weight loss and supported by the American College of Sports Medicine, the National Athletic Trainers' Association, and the Academy of Nutrition and Dietetics.

FLUID INTAKE FOR ENDURANCE ATHLETES

Hydrate before activity and every 15 minutes during activity. Then rehydrate afterward according to water weight loss.

Timing	Fluid Intake
Before activity	2 hours prior: 16 oz. (0.5l) 15 minutes prior: 8 to 16 oz. (0.25 to 0.5l)
During activity	4 to 16 oz. (.15 to .5l) per 15 minutes of activity
After activity	24 oz. (0.75l) per pound of body weight lost during activity

FAT RECOMMENDATIONS

Fats provide an additional source of energy for endurance athletes. Overconsumption of calories from fat, particularly saturated fats and cholesterol, may increase the risk of chronic diseases while contributing to obesity. Recommendations for fat intake range from 20 to 35 percent of total calorie intake, and limiting saturated fat intake to 10 percent of total calories. Endurance athletes should consume no less than 15 percent of total calorie intake from fats to prevent deficiencies.

SPORTS DRINKS
Sports drinks are an efficient source of hydration. Make your own using the recipes in this book.

Nutrition for **Strength Athletes**

Similar to endurance athletes, strength athletes need to focus on low-fiber foods 1 or 2 hours before physical activity and consume high-fiber foods 3 to 5 hours prior to physical activity to minimize any GI complications.

AVOIDING FAT

Intake of high-fat foods immediately before, during, or just after physical activity isn't recommended because these foods can decrease the rate of gastric emptying, which could delay the metabolism of nutrients and energy production; decrease the rate of glycogen synthesis; and cause GI complications like nausea, vomiting, diarrhea, or constipation.

DIETARY NEEDS FOR STRENGTH ATHLETES

Adjust fiber, carb, protein, and fat according to how much time there is before the activity.

Timing	Nutrient Needs
3 to 5 hours before exercise	High fiber, high carb, high protein, moderate fat
1 or 2 hours before exercise	Low fiber, high carb, low protein, low fat
Immediately before exercise	High carb, low protein, low fiber, low fat
Immediately after exercise	High carb, low to moderate protein, low fiber, low fat

WHAT CARBS SHOULD YOU EAT WHEN?

Carbohydrate recommendations when you're participating in strength training depend on the intensity and duration of your activity.

Consuming easily digested carbohydrate immediately before strength training won't provide you with an extra burst of energy, resulting in harder exercising. Instead, focus on building up your muscle and liver glycogen stores before physical activity as well as increasing your muscle creatine phosphate stores.

The following recommendations for carbohydrate intake for strength athletes are based on studies by Louise Burke, department head of sports nutrition at the Australian Institute of Sport.

CARBOHYDRATE NEEDS FOR STRENGTH ATHLETES

Recommended carb intake varies according to activity level.

Situation	Daily Needs
Normal strength sports	6 to 10g per kg body weight
Activity lasting 4 hours or longer	7 to 11g per kg body weight
Off season	5 to 7g per kg body weight

BREAD
Sandwiches made with whole-wheat bread, low-fat lunchmeat, and vegetables are an easy way to meet needs 3 to 5 hours before activity.

PASTA
Macaroni is a popular source of carbs. Top it with cheese for an easy protein boost.

TIMING YOUR CARB INTAKE

As a strength athlete, you should consume your last big meal 3 to 5 hours before competition. This may help replenish glycogen stores to sustain blood glucose levels for maintaining performance. Carbohydrate intake in the days leading up to a competition helps replenish muscle glycogen stores, whereas carbohydrate intake 1 or 2 hours prior to a competition mainly helps replenish your liver glycogen stores and has little effect on your muscle glycogen stores. Consuming carbohydrate 30 to 60 minutes before your event can be beneficial to building up liver glycogen stores and provide carbohydrate to maintain your blood glucose levels, but it might have some drawbacks as well.

In a study by William Sherman, exercise physiology expert, he recommends the following for carbohydrate intake during activity.

CARBS BEFORE AND DURING ACTIVITY

Intake before activity depends on body weight, whereas intake during activity is determined by length of exercise.

CARBOHYDRATE INTAKE PRIOR TO ACTIVITY

Hours Before Exercise	Recommended Carb Intake
1	1g per kg body weight
2	2g per kg body weight
3	3g per kg body weight
4	4g per kg body weight

CARBOHYDRATE INTAKE DURING ACTIVITY

Interval	Recommended Carb Intake
Every hour of activity	30 to 60 grams

MINIMIZING COMPLICATIONS AND MAXIMIZING PERFORMANCE

The amount and timing of carbohydrate intake prior to your activity is important for you to consider to minimize potential GI complications. A meal 2 to 4 hours before physical activity can help prevent hunger, which may distract you and impair your performance. Meal replacement beverages may be a good alternative and might not cause potential GI complications because they empty from your stomach faster than solid foods.

Carbohydrate intake is recommended during physical activity lasting 1 hour or longer to improve performance and delay fatigue. Carbohydrate intake during activity may provide an immediate fuel source, sparing your liver and muscle glycogen until absolutely necessary and promoting glycogen synthesis during rest periods. Some studies have shown improved performance benefits with stop-and-go sports like football, basketball, soccer, and tennis. Try to focus on easily digestible low-fiber foods like bagels, English muffins, crackers, graham crackers, and fruit juice or sports replacement beverages.

Carbohydrate intake is needed within 30 to 60 minutes during the recovery phase after activity.

CARBOHYDRATE INTAKE AFTER ACTIVITY LASTING 90 MINUTES OR LONGER

John Ivy, PhD, developed the following recommendations for carb intake after exercise.

Timing	Recommended Carb Intake
Within 30 minutes	1.5g per kg body weight
2 hours later	1.5g per kg body weight

PACKING ON MUSCLE WITH PROTEIN

Your protein needs increase with strength training due to the synthesis of new muscle and supporting connective tissue like collagen and contractile proteins like actin and myosin. As a strength athlete, you're in a constant flux of protein synthesis and protein breakdown. Protein needs also increase due to increased muscle mass, increased muscle hypertrophy, and synthesis of enzymes needed for anaerobic metabolism to meet the energy demands of strength training. These increased protein needs are particularly high during the first 3 to 6 months of training due to muscle hypertrophy adaptations.

Some studies, however, suggest that as you become trained, your body becomes more efficient at protein metabolism, which results in your body using less protein. Basically, the better trained you are, the less protein your body uses to build and maintain muscle and all its components, resulting in the need to consume less protein compared to the first 3 to 6 months of training. Most strength athletes believe they need more protein than is actually required and often consume more than they need.

Some drawbacks of overconsumption of protein include the following:

- You might get full on protein foods and not consume adequate carbohydrates to rebuild your glycogen stores.

- A high-protein diet can often be high in fat as well, resulting in extra calorie intake and potential weight gain.

- Animal protein foods are often expensive compared to plant-based protein food sources.

Protein can make up as much as 10 to 15 percent of your daily energy needs. Rates of protein breakdown are higher after physical activity than rates of protein synthesis. Protein is needed during recovery to promote the synthesis of new muscle protein and help repair damaged muscle proteins as a result of your training. Protein intake during recovery stimulates the rates of protein synthesis to be greater than the rates of protein breakdown, resulting in a net gain of protein synthesis and minimizing the impact of protein breakdown as a result of physical activity. Consuming carbohydrate with some protein during recovery may help you rebuild your muscle glycogen stores.

Position paper statements endorsed by the Academy of Nutrition and Dietetics and the American College of Sports Medicine recommend the following protein intake requirements.

STRENGTH TRAINING PROTEIN REQUIREMENTS

Top sports medicine associations make the following recommendations for daily protein intake and recovery requirements, both of which are based on weight.

Timing of Protein Intake	Requirements
Daily	1.5 to 1.7g per kg body weight per day
Recovery	0.1 to 0.2g per kg body weight per hour

Look for recipes in this book marked with this icon, denoting good sources of protein:

HIGH PROTEIN

HYDRATION FOR MUSCLES

As a strength athlete, you have higher fluid needs due to increased fluid losses from extra urine output resulting from protein metabolism. Protein contains nitrogen, which your body doesn't use, so it's concentrated and excreted from your body through your urine output. Consuming large amounts of protein results in increased amounts of nitrogen, which increases urine excretion and puts you at risk for dehydration. As little as a 1 or 2 percent weight decrease due to dehydration can impact your performance levels.

In studies, Edward Coyle, professor of exercise science at University of Texas at Austin, concluded that a 5 percent reduction or more of weight due to dehydration can decrease your performance by as much as 30 percent. As you become dehydrated, you also can become fatigued and suffer from reduced concentration, which might increase your risk of injury during training or competition.

SPORTS DRINKS

Sports replacement beverages are a great way to maintain hydration during and after physical activity. They supply carbohydrate for energy and contain sodium, which can help prevent dehydration during and improve rehydration after physical activity. This book includes recipes for many delicious sports drinks you can make yourself.

FLUID RECOMMENDATIONS

The following current recommendations for fluid replacement for athletes are supported by the American College of Sports Medicine, the National Athletic Trainers' Association, and the Academy of Nutrition and Dietetics.

FLUID INTAKE FOR ENDURANCE ATHLETES

Hydrate prior to activity based on body weight, during activity based on length of activity, and afterward based on water weight lost.

Timing	Fluid Intake
2 hours before activity	7ml per kg actual body weight or 1 oz. (30ml) for every 10 lb. (4.5kg) body weight
20 minutes prior to activity (for hot environments and heavy sweating expected)	Additional 3 or 4ml per kg actual body weight or 0.6 oz. (17ml) for every 10 lb. (4.5kg) body weight
During activity	24 oz. to 50 oz. (750ml to 1.5l) per hour of activity (for light to heavy sweaters)
After activity	24 oz. (750ml) for each pound lost during activity

TAKE-ALONG HYDRATION
Adequate fluid intake is essential before, during, and after strength training.

The Gluten-Free **Athlete**

Gluten is a general term used for proteins found in wheat, rye, and barley that give elasticity to dough but also have been related to food allergies and food sensitivities. Wheat gluten is typically found in breads, baked goods, soups, pasta, cereals, sauces, and salad dressings. Other sources of gluten include rye bread, pumpernickel, and barley found in malt, soups, beer, and malt vinegar.

THE BENEFITS OF A GLUTEN-FREE DIET

Many athletes eat a gluten-free diet and claim it helps their performance. Eliminating gluten may ease digestive symptoms during competition like nausea, vomiting, abdominal cramping, bloating, diarrhea, and constipation. Better digestion also can aid nutrient absorption, which can help improve performance.

A gluten-free diet has been suggested to be anti-inflammatory. Less inflammation can lead to reduced joint pain and improved muscle performance. It also can expedite the healing process and promote recovery.

Gluten-free foods can be higher in fiber and l ess processed, which can help improve blood glucose control and prevent episodes of hypoglycemia. Currently, however, there is no research supporting claims regarding a gluten-free diet and any improvements in athletic performance.

MAXIMIZING PERFORMANCE ON A GLUTEN-FREE DIET

Most bread, grains, rice, pasta, and cereals are required to be fortified with various nutrients such as vitamins and minerals that may be lost during processing to ensure nutritional standards are met. Gluten-free products are not required to be fortified and, therefore, may be lacking several nutrients that are important for athletes. Gluten-free foods may be inadequate in iron, calcium, vitamin D, magnesium, zinc, folate, B_{12}, niacin, riboflavin, and thiamine.

Many gluten-free products also contain more calories in the form of fat and sugar compared to the regular versions, which could contribute to unnecessary weight gain. Focus on naturally gluten-free foods like vegetables, fruits, legumes, and gluten-free whole grains; read food labels, looking for "gluten free" on packaging; and read the allergen statement on food labels for hidden forms of gluten.

FINDING HIDDEN GLUTEN

The U.S. Food and Drug Administration requires that a product must contain fewer than 20 parts per million (ppm) of gluten to be labeled "gluten free." Be sure to read the ingredient list and look at the bottom of the food label for allergen warnings or a list of potential allergens the product may contain, such as wheat, soy, milk, eggs, or peanuts. Remember, if wheat isn't

CHOOSING GRAINS

Many viable alternatives to wheat and other gluten-containing grains are available.

GLUTEN-FREE GRAINS AND SEEDS

Amaranth	Montina
Arrowroot	Quinoa
Bean flours	Rice
Buckwheat	Seed flours
Corn	Sorghum
Flax	Tapioca
Millet	Teff
Nut flours	

listed on the allergen warning line, it might not mean the product is gluten free—just that the product is *wheat* free. Read the ingredient list closely to find other possible sources of gluten.

AVOIDING CROSS-CONTAMINATION

Avoid consuming gluten by accident by preventing cross contamination, or contaminating a safe, gluten-free product with gluten. This can happen by using gluten-free bread in a toaster or on a cutting board that has been used for white or wheat breads. Using a knife on a gluten-containing food to spread a condiment and dipping it back in a container, for example, could cross contaminate that product. To avoid cross-contamination, store foods separately and remember to clean pots, pans, utensils, and countertops thoroughly.

AVOIDING HIDDEN GLUTEN

If you are new to a gluten-free diet, be particularly aware of these foods that contain unexpected gluten.

FOODS THAT MAY CONTAIN HIDDEN GLUTEN

Beer, ale, lagers	Malted milk
Brewer's yeast	Modified food starch (containing wheat)
Candies (some)	
Cheeses (some)	Potato and tortilla chips (some)
Deli meats (some)	Processed meats (premade hamburgers, meatloaf, Salisbury steak)
Flavorings	
Gravies	Salad dressings
Imitation bacon bits	Soups
Imitation seafood	Soy sauce
Malt vinegar	Teriyaki sauce

RICE
When you're not sure what to eat on a gluten-free diet, remember the acronym *CPR*, for *corn, potatoes,* and *rice.* Foods made from these grains, and without any gluten-based additives, are safe to eat.

Feeding a **Family of Athletes**

Feeding yourself, or a family of athletes, is no easy task. You already have a packed schedule with your job, intense workouts, and competitions, and you still have to shop, mind your budget, and make dinner. In this section, we share a quick and easy weekly meal plan.

SALTY SNACKS

Snacks containing sodium are a great way to help prevent dehydration and promote rehydration after physical activity. Try to keep a few salty snacks on hand, such as popcorn, pretzels, and nuts. Soups, sports drinks, and trail mix bars also are good to consume. (Try our Lentil Soup, Maryland Vegetable Crab Soup, or Sweet and Salty Peanut Bars.)

GETTING YOUR CARBS

Carbohydrates are an athlete's main fuel, and your body can use them immediately for energy or store them as glycogen for later use. Good sources of carbs include grains and seeds like rice, pasta, noodles, bread, cereal, beans, potatoes, and quinoa. (Try our Homemade Hamburger Casserole, Shrimp and Spinach Pasta, or Garlic Chicken with Orzo Pasta.)

SAMPLE ONE-WEEK MENU (Per Person; Does Not Include Fluids or Caloric Intake)

Meal	Sunday	Monday	Tuesday
Breakfast	1 serving Blueberry Orange Parfaits	1 serving Baked Country Ham, Egg, and Cheese Cups	1 serving Coffeecake Power Muffins
Snack	1 serving Sparkling Apple Cinnamon Refresher	1 cup low-fat Greek yogurt, 1 cup fresh berries	1 cup fresh vegetables, 4 tablespoons low-fat dip
Lunch (3 or 4 hours before training/competition)	1 serving Turkey and Scallion Wraps, 1 small side salad	1 serving Classic Chef Salad, 1 small roll	1 serving Carb-Loaded Bean and Vegetable Soup, ½ sandwich
Snack (1 hour before training/competition)	1 serving Sweet and Salty Peanut Bars	¼ cup whole roasted almonds, ½ cup fresh strawberries	1 cup low-fat Greek yogurt, 1 small plum
Training/Competition	1 serving Gingerade	1 serving Acai Punch	1 serving Quick and Easy Energy Bars
Dinner (30 minutes to 1 hour after training/competion)	1 serving Homemade Hamburger Casserole, 1 side salad	1 serving Garlic Chicken with Orzo Pasta, 1 side salad	1 serving Slow Cooker Corned Beef and Cabbage
Snack	2 tablespoons peanut butter, 1 serving crackers	1 serving Bran Raisin Cookies	1 cup mixed fruit

PACKING THE PROTEIN

Protein is essential for athletes for building and maintaining muscle. Shop for lean cuts of beef and pork; skinless chicken and turkey; and ground turkey breast instead of the fattier ground turkey. And try to eat fish once or twice a week. Limit processed meats like bacon, sausage, bologna, and hot dogs.

You can buy in bulk and portion out meats to freeze until needed. Canned chicken, turkey, and tuna are always good to have on hand for quick protein-packed meal preparation. Try to use leftover meats in casseroles, soups, or stews, or make items like chicken or turkey salads for sandwiches. To save time, bake a chicken, pork roast, etc. early in the week and use the meat in various preparations for several days.

Nut butters as well as beans and legumes also are good protein foods to have in your pantry. They keep for a long time and can be used in many different dishes to add a little extra protein and carbs.

Also try using tofu and seitan in recipes as great meat alternatives.

Wednesday	Thursday	Friday	Saturday
1 serving Egg and Avocado Breakfast Burritos	1 serving Green Monster Smoothie	1 serving Orange Ginger Muffins	1 serving Peaches and Cream Smoothie
1 small banana, ¼ cup cashews	1 serving Chocolate Peanut Butter Bars	1 serving reduced-fat pretzels with 2 servings hummus	¼ cup whole roasted almonds, ½ cup fresh blackberries
1 serving Reduced-Fat Tuna Melts, 1 side salad	1 serving Whole-Wheat Turkey and Veggie Pita Sandwich, 1 serving Greek Pasta Salad	1 serving Cobb salad, 1 cup chicken noodle soup	1 serving Mediterranean Salmon Wraps, 1 cup diced fruit
1 medium peach, 1 serving graham crackers	1 medium apple, 2 tablespoons peanut butter	1 cup fresh vegetables, 4 tablespoons low-fat dip	2 clementines, 2 ounces (55g) reduced-fat cheese
1 serving Blackberry Cooler	1 serving Cranberry Limeade	1 serving Pineapple Ginger Sipper	1 serving Lavender Lemonade Relaxer
1 serving Stuffed Zucchini Boats, 1 cup rice	1 serving Spaghetti with Meat Sauce, 1 small roll, 1 side salad	1 serving Easy Slow Cooker Pot Roast variation with vegetables	1 serving Lentil Soup, 1 small roll, 1 side salad
1 serving Black Bean Brownies	¾ cup reduced-fat frozen Greek yogurt, ¼ cup blueberries	1 serving Blueberry Madness Bars	1 cup strawberries, 1 serving reduced-fat whipped topping

Top 10
Superfoods for Athletes

In addition to other protein sources such as meat, and carb sources, keep these must-have items on hand to make quick and powerful meals for you and your family.

Dairy Calcium is needed for proper muscle function as well as building strong bones. Focus on low- or reduced-fat or fat-free dairy products like milk, yogurts, or cheeses. (Use Greek yogurt for extra protein for our Orange Creamcicles recipe.)

Nuts Nuts are a great source of protein and vitamin E, which is important for cardiac health and as an antioxidant. Try raw or roasted nuts like cashews and walnuts, or spread nut butters like peanut butter or almond butter on whole-wheat bread or on fruit as a snack. (Have cashews on hand for our Quick and Easy Energy Bars; peanuts for our Sweet and Salty Peanut Bars; peanut butter for our Chocolate Peanut Butter Bars; and almonds, Brazil nuts, and hazelnuts for our Homemade Tropical Snack Mix.)

Red fruits and vegetables Red-colored foods contain lycopene, a phytonutrient that has antioxidant-like properties and has been associated with decreased risk of cancers such as prostate, breast, and cervical. Focus on red fruits and vegetables like red tomatoes, cherries, red bell peppers, beets, pomegranates, and watermelon. (Use diced tomatoes in our Chickpea, Tomato, and Pasta Soup.)

Blue and purple fruits and vegetables Blue- and purple-colored foods contain compounds called lutein, zeaxanthin, and resveratrol as well as vitamin C, which have antioxidant-like properties. Add blueberries to cereals, salads, and smoothies, and work blackberries, eggplant, purple cabbage, and raisins into your diet. (Try our Acai Punch.)

CHEESE NUTS TOMATOES BLUEBERRIES BROCCOLI

Green fruits and vegetables   Green-colored foods contain lutein and zeaxanthin, both of which promote eye health. Green fruits and vegetables are also high in vitamins C and A. Try asparagus, avocados, broccoli, honeydew, and kiwi fruit. (Go green with our Green Monster Smoothie.)

Seafood   Seafood is an excellent source of protein as well as zinc, which is needed in several energy pathways in the body and for proper immune function. Some seafood can also be good sources of omega-3 fatty acids, such as cold-water fish like salmon, herring, mackerel, sardines, and tuna. Other sources of omega-3 fatty acids include eggs, nuts, seeds, and oils. (Blackened Tilapia, anyone?)

Yellow and orange fruits and vegetables   Yellow- and orange-colored foods contain beta-carotene, lycopene, potassium, vitamin A, and vitamin C. Try apricots, cantaloupe, grapefruit, mangoes, nectarines, oranges, papaya, pumpkin, and sweet potatoes. (Refresh yourself with our Mango Cooler.)

Beans and legumes   Beans and legumes are great sources of protein and fiber and can help you feel full longer. They're also low in fat, contain no cholesterol, and can help reduce LDL (bad) cholesterol. Stock lentils, chickpeas, lima beans, black beans, pinto beans, and kidney beans, and add them to salads, casseroles, soups, and chilies. (Sneak in some protein with our Black Bean Brownies.)

Soy   Soy is a versatile food you can enjoy as edamame, tofu, and soymilk. Soy can help lower cholesterol and reduce the risk of osteoporosis and is high in isoflavones, an antioxidant. (Tofu is a great meat alternative and is used in several recipes in the book.)

Oats   Oats are high in soluble fiber, which can help reduce LDL cholesterol. They're high in carbohydrate, various B vitamins, and an antioxidant called avenanthramides. Try adding fruit to oatmeal or adding oats to smoothies. (Wake up to our delicious Whole-Wheat Oatmeal Pancakes.)

FISH   ORANGES   BLACK-EYED PEAS   SOYBEANS   OATS

Stocking **Your Kitchen**

Great cooking requires organization and planning. Having a well-stocked kitchen is essential to preparing meals quickly and easily and with the right nutrients to fuel your body.

IN THE PANTRY
Proteins

Canned seafood   Choose canned tuna, salmon, or shellfish, packed in water instead of oil to cut extra calories. Opt for chunk light tuna because it typically contains less mercury than solid white tuna.

Canned beans   These are a great source of protein and fiber. Just drain and rinse, and you can add them to salads, soups, and casseroles or enjoy them as a side dish. Choose black, navy, pinto, kidney, chickpeas, lentils, and others.

Nuts and nut butters   Almonds, walnuts, pecans, etc. (Although these do have a higher fat component in addition to the protein, they offer healthy fats as well as extra calories to meet your needs.)

Carbs

Breads   Whole-wheat, rye, bagels, tortillas, pitas, English muffins.

Grains, seeds, and pastas   Rice, barley, quinoa, oats, breadcrumbs, farfalle, orzo, couscous.

Fruits and Vegetables

Tomatoes (canned)   Whole, diced, chopped, stewed, paste, sauce.

Fruit (canned and dried)   Peaches, pears, pineapple, apricots, cherries.

Potatoes   Russet, red, Yukon, sweet.

SAVE TIME AND EAT BETTER
Keep your pantry organized, or at least try to. Simplifying and organizing your cooking environment not only saves you time in the kitchen, but also makes cooking a much less daunting task.

Shop local and seasonal when you can. The best foods you can stock are those that fuel your body and satisfy your taste buds. Try new ingredients to spice up your routine, and keep a variety of basic ingredients on hand so you're ready to tackle any recipe that sparks your interest.

PECANS   OLIVE OIL

Extras

Sugars and sweeteners   Brown, granulated, confectioners', honey, agave.

Oils   Olive, canola, vegetable, pan sprays.

Herbs and spices   Oregano, basil, parsley, rosemary, cumin, bay leaves, thyme, cilantro, tarragon, chives, dill, cinnamon, nutmeg, paprika, mustard, ginger, allspice, garlic, black pepper.

Salt   Salt comes in many different forms, but in the recipes in this book, we used mostly regular table salt.

Baking ingredients   Baking powder, baking soda, cornstarch, chocolate chips, evaporated milk, vanilla extract.

Condiments   Ketchup, mustard, mayonnaise, horseradish.

Sauces   Marinara, Worcestershire, hot sauce, oyster sauce, soy sauce.

Vinegars   White, apple cider, balsamic.

IN THE REFRIGERATOR

Meat   Chicken, beef, pork, seafood.

Lean deli meats   All-natural turkey, chicken, or ham make for quick sandwiches or snacks. Look for deli meats with no added preservatives, nitrates, or nitrites.

Rotisserie chicken   You can purchase these already cooked at supermarkets or large wholesaler stores. They're a great quick and easy meal, and you can use the leftovers for soups, stews, or casseroles—or just to make a sandwich.

Dairy products   Milk, yogurt, cheeses. (Milk and yogurt have the bonus of protein in addition to their carb component—a double whammy. Choose low-fat or reduced-fat items when appropriate.)

Butters   Salted and unsalted.

CHOCOLATE CHIPS   ORZO PASTA   DRIED FRUIT

Top 10 Kitchen Tools
for Athletes

Having the proper utensils not only saves you time in the kitchen, but also takes the extra work out of food preparation. These kitchen essentials will get a lot of use in your kitchen.

1 MEASURING CUPS AND SPOONS

Every recipe requires precise dry or liquid measurements. Get a set of metal or plastic cups for measuring dry ingredients. For measuring liquid ingredients, a 4- to 8-cup capacity cup suffices.

2 MUFFIN PAN

A baking pan with 6 or 12 cups holds muffin or cupcake batter, or the egg cup recipes in this book.

3 BAKING PAN/ CASSEROLE DISH

A 9×13-inch (23×33cm) dish is great for making casseroles or baking dessert bars, brownies, and cakes to take along to events or store for later.

4 SCALE

Ideal for measuring ingredients accurately.

5

BLENDER/JUICER
Great for making sports drinks, smoothies, milkshakes, fresh juice, salad dressings, and even some soups.

6

FOOD PROCESSER
This versatile piece of equipment can chop, slice, shred, and purée, saving lots of time in the kitchen.

7

SLOW COOKER
This handy appliance cooks appetizers, meals, barbecue, chili, soups, stews, side dishes, and even desserts over a longer period of time. Put ingredients into it in the morning, and come home after your workout to a ready meal.

8

MICROWAVE
Microwaves heat quickly and efficiently and are great for defrosting, cooking, and heating up leftovers.

9

TOASTER OVEN
This handy appliance performs as a traditional toaster but also can bake or broil foods. It's great for warming up egg cups and other leftovers that are best when crispy.

10

IMMERSION BLENDER
This frequently used appliance blends in the pan and can be used to mix up a smoothie quickly and easily.

Quick-Cooking and Meal-Assembly Tips

Busy school, work, and training schedules mean there's not always a lot of time to spend in the kitchen. Here are some hints for making the most of your time while preparing wholesome food that will fuel your athlete's body.

QUICK-COOKING METHODS

Grilling   Grilling cooks food quickly over high heat and adds flavor. Be sure the grill is preheated and ready, whether it's a gas or charcoal grill.

Microwaving   Heats up leftovers and provides quick thawing. Many microwaves come with programmed times for commonly cooked foods.

Stir-frying   Cook small pieces of food quickly over high heat in a small amount of oil. The food must be constantly stirred to evenly distribute heat and avoid overcooking.

Steaming   This method of cooking is quick and generally healthier for you because it preserves nutrients better. Steaming is a great way to prepare vegetables and even fish. Steaming using parchment paper is another great way to prepare chicken, fish, and vegetables.

Sautéing or pan-frying   This high-heat cooking method is great for cooking meats and searing in juices. Remember to preheat the pan before adding oil, butter, or a cooking spray. Don't add additional foods too early, or the heat in the pan won't distribute evenly and food won't be cooked thoroughly. After sautéing meat, add a little bit of liquid like water or broth to make gravy.

Broiling   This method quickly cooks tender meats and vegetables on a broiler pan. Remember to arrange the oven racks so the food is the right distance away from the heat source.

Pressure cooking   This method cooks food quickly by increasing the pressure in the locked container and boiling the food at a high temperature. Most new models are digital and have safety features.

Poaching   This method uses liquid heated just under boiling to simmer foods such as eggs, fruits, and some meats.

STIR-FRYING
Stir-frying is fast and tasty way to cook proteins and vegetables together for a satisfying meal.

SLOW COOKING
Although it's not quick per se, slow cooking is a timesaving cooking method for busy days. Simply toss everything in the slow cooker, set it to low, and your dish will be ready when you get home (usually in 6 to 8 hours).

Prepping and **Planning Ahead**

Planning ahead and spending some time preparing are the keys to eating quick, healthy meals. Here are some tips that will save you time during your weekday meal preparation:

Thaw frozen food by removing it from the freezer and thawing it in the refrigerator 12 to 24 hours prior to use. If you're short on time, use the microwave to defrost quickly.

Cut fresh vegetables, and store them in containers for quick use. You can also buy precut vegetables, but they cost more. Chopped vegetables such as onions, carrots, broccoli, cauliflower, and peppers store well in the refrigerator for several days. Potatoes tend to turn brown after a day. For best appearance and texture, wait until just before the meal to chop salad greens.

PREPARED INGREDIENTS
Use your prep day to chop vegetables, cook grains and pastas, or make sauces, and store them in separate containers in the refrigerator for later in the week.

Cook big batches of ground meats such as beef, turkey, and chicken, or make hard-boiled eggs on the weekend to incorporate into meals throughout the week. Lean ground beef and ground turkey breast are great additions to sauces, soups, and chilies. Chicken can be sliced or diced and added to pasta, rice, soups, or salads. Hard-boiled eggs can be used sliced or chopped in salads or egg salad.

Cook large batches of grains and seeds like brown rice, barley, and quinoa for use within 3 or 4 days, or freeze.

Make a meal plan for the week. Have an idea of what you'll cook and when so you have ingredients prepared ahead of time and will know which days you'll be eating leftovers.

Speed up cleanup by lining your baking dishes or baking sheets with aluminum foil or parchment paper.

Designate shopping and prep days. Pick one day of the week as your grocery shopping day and one day as your plan and prep day. Use those days to get meals and ingredients ready for the rest of the week, saving time for busier days.

Use your kitchen appliances. Rice cookers, food processors, and slow cookers speed up meal prep and save you time.

Stay organized. Keep your pantry, refrigerator, freezer, and kitchen utensils clean and organized so you know where everything is to avoid wasting time looking for things. It's tempting to let the dishes pile up in the sink, but you save time in the long run if you fill your dishwasher after every meal.

DON'T LEAVE OUT THE LEFTOVERS
Skillful use of leftovers saves time and money. Here are our top hints:

- Increase recipes for 2 to make 4 or 8 servings, or scale down larger recipes to avoid making too much. To adjust recipes, check out an online calculator such as free-online-calculator-use.com/recipe-conversion-calculator.html#calculator or fruitfromwashington.com/Recipes/scale/recipeconversions.php.

- Store leftovers in small, shallow glass containers or microwave-safe containers.

- Use leftovers within 3 days; otherwise freeze for later use or throw away. Use frozen leftovers within 4 months.

- Be sure to heat leftovers to a minimal temperature of 165°F (75°C) to reduce the risk of food poisoning.

- When in doubt, throw it out. It's better to waste some food than make yourself sick.

Making **Portables**

Healthy portable dishes can play a major role in maintaining adequate nutritional intake. Distributing these calories throughout the day helps ensure your body has a steady stream of energy and is able to perform its best all day long.

One of the most difficult things about being an athlete is maintaining adequate nutrition. You work out hard and burn extreme amounts of calories, so it's important that you make time to replenish your nutrition throughout the day.

Experts agree that consuming six small meals throughout the course of the day is a better alternative than the standard breakfast, lunch, and dinner plan. Those smaller, more frequent meals ensure your body is being nourished all day long.

WHAT ARE PORTABLES?

Most likely, you've been taking advantage of portables for a while now and might not even be aware that you're doing so. Portables can be any kind of foods that are easily mobile and can be held at room temperature (ideally) for pre-, mid-, or post-event snacks. Some foods you might be familiar with are workout bars, trail mixes, gummy snacks, etc.

Ideally, portables are simple carbohydrates along with some protein and little fat that are easy for your body to break down and utilize on the go. Some portables are geared for different times in your workouts, so be sure to take a look at what you're eating so your body is able to get what it needs when it needs it.

In this book, we have three recipe sections, all of which contain recipes for various portables for different times in your workout—before, during, and after. We've put together some tasty, tested alternatives to store-bought items such as Baked Egg and Tomato Cups, Egg and Avocado Breakfast Burritos, Mediterranean Salmon Wraps, and Mini Sweet Potato Pies.

SNACK MIX CEREAL BARS
This high-carb, high-protein snack is ideal for taking along to events.

MAKING PORTABLES PORTABLE

We've included a number of fantastic portables in the recipes in this book, from bars, to baked eggs, to mini pies. To get these foods where you need to go, be sure you wrap them well. Use zipper-lock plastic bags for foods like cookies, trail mixes, and other snacks; enclose foods like wrap-style sandwiches, baked egg cups, and muffins in aluminum foil, parchment paper, or plastic wrap; or even tuck some foods in reusable containers, such as marinated salads, various sandwiches, or other food items that may be a little messier with travel. Use whatever suits your situation best.

In the recipes, we give suggestions on whether portables should be stored chilled or room temperature for travel. Keep these recommendations in mind when choosing how to wrap your portables and how to best travel with them.

Making Your Own **Sports Drinks** and **Smoothies**

Sports drinks are an excellent way to replenish lost fluids, electrolytes, and even excess calories burned during and after a good workout. Smoothies replace fluids but also have protein and extra carbs, so they are great with preevent meals.

Homemade sports drinks and smoothies are a great alternative to commercially made versions. You can create flavor combinations that suit your tastes and adjust the nutrient content to fit your body's needs. In addition, creating your own sports drinks and smoothies keeps the costs down compared to store-bought versions.

DIY SPORTS DRINKS

Sports drinks are probably the easiest replenishment beverage to prepare—and the least expensive. You can prepare these beverages ahead of time and store them in bottles, jugs, etc. until you're ready to drink them. Having a few bottles that are already filled in the refrigerator means you have a quick grab-and-go replenishing option whenever you need it. (Some of the recipes for sports drinks in this book are carbonated and will retain their bubbles better if the carbonated beverage is mixed in at time of consumption.)

WHAT'S GOOD AND BAD ABOUT COCONUT WATER
Coconut water has been called "nature's sports drink" because it has fewer calories than average sports drinks, less sodium, and more potassium. This is a great beverage option if you need more fluid and not as many carbs. The only drawback is the lower sodium, which is one of the main electrolytes your body loses when you sweat. The average American consumes more sodium than the recommended 1,500 to 2,000 milligrams per day, which can offset the limited amount ($\approx$5.45mg per ounce) found in coconut water. (Ask your doctor or dietitian how much sodium you need.)

There are three main types of sports drinks:
Isotonic sports drinks   These are designed to replace fluids lost from sweating, as well as provide extra carbohydrates for energy. Long-distance runners, or those who need extra fluids with a little carbohydrate boost in their daily workout routine, usually prefer these types of sports drinks.

Hypertonic sports drinks   These drinks help increase your overall carbohydrate intake. They contain high levels of carbohydrates and are used to maintain muscle glycogen stores. These beverages are used by marathoners or those who burn extreme amounts of calories and use these types of beverages to meet their body's energy requirements.

Hypotonic sports drinks   These drinks replace fluids lost through sweating, quickly, by providing mainly fluids in the beverage along with lower amounts of carbohydrates. These drinks are popular with athletes who need more hydration but do not need the extra carbs for extended events, such as gymnasts and weight lifters. Hypotonic sports drinks are most commonly used by everyday gym-goers to replenish their fluid losses.

One of the best reasons for making your own sports drinks is that you know what's in them. They're not going to be "flavored water," but rather are a combination of juice of your choice, water, and a little salt. What's not included are the color additives and undesirable preservatives often found in store-bought drinks.

SENSATIONAL SMOOTHIES

Smoothies are a superb option for packing fruits, vegetables, calories, and more in your diet, depending on what you need for your specific workout. Smoothies can be prepared quickly and easily with just a little preplanning and preparation.

Packed full of antioxidants, vitamins, and minerals your body needs to sustain intense workouts, smoothies are also helpful for carbohydrate-loading before your next big event.

The best part about a smoothie is that you can get in all these various necessary macro- and micronutrients without having to consume immense amounts of solid foods.

The typical smoothie starts with a base of protein, such as Greek yogurt, milk, or cottage cheese. Add to that fruits such as bananas for a smoother consistency, strawberries for taste and fiber, and oranges for vitamin C.

You also can add powerful vegetables such as spinach, broccoli, or kale, and you'll hardly notice them. Add some chia seeds for extra protein, and include some ice for coldness and texture. Put it all in the blender, and blend until smooth.

GREEN SMOOTHIES
Spinach not only turns your smoothie green, it also provides extra iron, protein, and fiber.

Recipes for
Training

When it comes to training for any sport, your body needs more fuel than normal to keep it moving, and proper nutrition and hydration give your body what it needs to perform optimally. In Part 2, we give you dozens of recipes that will give you energy for the best workouts of your life, from homemade sports drinks and smoothies to delicious portable meals, soups, salads, entrées, and desserts.

These aren't just your average preworkout recipes, either. The recipes in the following pages will be a hit with your entire family, and you can even take them along to share at sports-related functions, with friends at the gym, or at your kid's next practice.

We know you're going to love these great, high-powered training recipes.

2

Lavender Lemonade **Relaxer**

This summery lemonade has a subtle hint of lavender.

  Easy

PREP 2 hours, 10 mins
COOK about 5 mins

YIELD 1 serving

INGREDIENTS

⅓ cup sugar
⅓ cup water
⅛ cup dried lavender flowers
½ cup lemon juice
1 cup cold water
⅛ tsp. salt

1 In small saucepan over medium-high heat, bring sugar and water to a boil. Add lavender flowers, remove from heat, and set aside for 2 hours. Strain syrup, and discard lavender.

2 Stir in lemon juice, water, and salt, and serve over ice.

NUTRITION PER SERVING

CALORIES	190
CARBOHYDRATES	59g
SUGARS	51g
DIETARY FIBER	0g
PROTEIN	0g
FAT	0g
CHOLESTEROL	0g
SODIUM	300mg
VITAMIN C	90%
VITAMIN A	0%
IRON	0%

Coco Melon Lime **Cooler**

This sports drink is a little sweet and very refreshing—perfect for a long day of training.

 Easy

PREP 5 mins

YIELD 1 serving

INGREDIENTS

1 cup cubed watermelon
1 cup coconut water
Juice of ¼ lime (about 1½ tsp.)

1 In a blender, combine watermelon, coconut water, and lime juice until smooth.

2 Drink immediately.

NUTRITION PER SERVING

CALORIES	90
CARBOHYDRATES	25g
SUGARS	19g
DIETARY FIBER	4g
PROTEIN	2g
FAT	0g
CHOLESTEROL	0g
SODIUM	260mg
VITAMIN C	35%
VITAMIN A	10%
IRON	6%

Ginger Lime **Energizer**

Cool and refreshing, this energizing beverage with sweet honey and tart lime will keep you going!

 Easy

PREP 5 mins

YIELD 1 serving

INGREDIENTS

¾ cup ginger soda
1½ TB. honey
Juice of 1 medium lime (2 TB.)
⅛ tsp. salt

1 In a large glass, combine ginger soda, honey, lime juice, and salt.

2 Drink over ice immediately.

NUTRITION PER SERVING

CALORIES	160
CARBOHYDRATES	45g
SUGARS	41g
DIETARY FIBER	0g
PROTEIN	0g
FAT	0g
CHOLESTEROL	0g
SODIUM	310mg
VITAMIN C	15%
VITAMIN A	0%
IRON	0%

Coco Melon
Lime Cooler

Lavender
Lemonade Relaxer

Ginger Lime Energizer

Blackberry **Cooler**

This sweet drink features fresh summer blackberries with a hint of mint. Coconut water adds to the fresh flavor.

  Easy

PREP 5 mins

YIELD 1 serving

INGREDIENTS

4 fresh mint leaves
5 fresh blackberries
2 tsp. honey
Juice of ½ lemon (about 1 TB.)
½ cup club soda
¼ cup coconut water

1 In a large glass, combine mint and blackberries, and press together with the back of a spoon until blackberries are crushed.

2 Stir in honey, lemon juice, club soda, and coconut water.

3 Drink over ice immediately.

NUTRITION PER SERVING	
CALORIES	90
CARBOHYDRATES	23g
SUGARS	16g
DIETARY FIBER	5g
PROTEIN	2g
FAT	0g
CHOLESTEROL	0g
SODIUM	65mg
VITAMIN C	50%
VITAMIN A	4%
IRON	4%

Acai **Punch**

This cool and refreshing punch, flavored with sweet honey and tangy lime, will keep you energized!

  Easy

PREP 5 mins

YIELD 1 serving

INGREDIENTS

4 fresh mint leaves
⅛ tsp. salt
2 lime wedges
¾ cup acai juice
¼ cup water

1 In a large glass, combine mint, salt, and lime wedges, and press together with the back of a spoon until salt starts to dissolve in lime juice.

2 Pour in acai juice and water, and combine.

3 Enjoy immediately over ice.

NUTRITION PER SERVING	
CALORIES	90
CARBOHYDRATES	21g
SUGARS	20g
DIETARY FIBER	0g
PROTEIN	0g
FAT	0g
CHOLESTEROL	0g
SODIUM	55mg
VITAMIN C	130%
VITAMIN A	0%
IRON	8%

Super-Easy **Sports Drink**

Make this simple sports drink with any fruit or vegetable juice in minutes!

   Easy

PREP 2 mins

YIELD 12 servings

INGREDIENTS

2 qt. (2l) any flavor juice
1 qt. (1l) water
½ tsp. salt

1 In a pitcher, combine juice, water, and salt.

2 Refrigerate for up to 1 week.

NUTRITION PER SERVING	
CALORIES	45
CARBOHYDRATES	12g
SUGARS	11g
DIETARY FIBER	0g
PROTEIN	0g
FAT	0g
CHOLESTEROL	0g
SODIUM	110mg
VITAMIN C	70%
VITAMIN A	15%
IRON	0%

Super-Easy Sports Drink

Blackberry Cooler

Acai Punch

Baked Country Ham, Egg, and Cheese **Cups**

This is a great grab-and-go recipe you can bake ahead of time and take with you anywhere. With sweet potato and delicious country ham, it's sure to become one of your portable favorites.

● ● ○ ○   **Easy**

PREP 10 mins
COOK about 45 mins

YIELD 12 servings

INGREDIENTS

1 medium sweet potato,
    washed, peeled, and shredded
1 tsp. extra-virgin olive oil
½ tsp. sea salt
¼ tsp. freshly cracked
    black pepper
12 large eggs
4 oz. (110g) country ham,
    roughly chopped
½ cup shredded sharp
    cheddar cheese

1 Preheat the oven to 350°F (180°C). Lightly grease a 12-cup muffin pan with cooking spray.

2 In a small bowl, combine sweet potato with extra-virgin olive oil, sea salt, and black pepper.

3 Evenly divide sweet potato mixture among the muffin tins and pat down a bit to make a crust.

4 Bake sweet potato mixture for 15 to 20 minutes or until sweet potato starts to brown.

5 Remove muffin tins from the oven, and crack 1 egg into each tin. Evenly distribute chopped country ham and sharp cheddar cheese over top of each egg.

6 Return muffin tins to the oven for 20 to 25 minutes or until eggs are firm.

7 Allow eggs to cool to room temperature before serving.

8 Store leftover eggs in a zipper-lock plastic bag in the refrigerator or freezer. Reheat in the oven or microwave when needed.

Make ahead and freeze: Refrigerate after step 8 for up to 5 days, or freeze for up to 2 months.

This is a great base recipe you can adapt to make many different types of baked egg cups. Try making vegetarian options with spinach and goat cheese or diced vegetables.

NUTRITION PER SERVING			
CALORIES	110	FAT	6g
CARBOHYDRATES	3g	CHOLESTEROL	220mg
SUGARS	1g	SODIUM	440mg
DIETARY FIBER	1g	VITAMIN C	2%
PROTEIN	11g	VITAMIN A	45%
		IRON	6%

Egg and Avocado
Breakfast Burritos

You can make these breakfast burritos ahead of time and heat them in a toaster oven or microwave when you're ready to eat. They're full of protein from the egg plus healthy fats from the avocado.

● ● ● **Easy**

PREP 5 mins
COOK 7 mins

YIELD 4 servings

INGREDIENTS

6 large eggs
1 TB. extra-virgin olive oil
¼ medium red onion, diced small (about ¼ cup)
4 (6-in.; 15.25cm) wheat tortillas
¼ cup salsa
2 small avocados, peeled, seeded, and sliced

1 In a medium bowl, whisk together eggs. Set aside.

2 In a medium skillet over medium-low heat, sauté red onion for about 1 or 2 minutes or until tender.

3 Pour eggs into the skillet, and scramble for about 4 or 5 minutes or until eggs are cooked through.

4 Evenly divide egg mixture among wheat tortillas, and top each serving with 1 tablespoon salsa and sliced avocado equivalent to about ½ avocado.

5 Roll tortillas around filling, and enjoy.

To make this recipe gluten free, use gluten-free tortillas.

NUTRITION PER SERVING			
CALORIES	450	FAT	6g
CARBOHYDRATES	34g	CHOLESTEROL	315mg
SUGARS	4g	SODIUM	370mg
DIETARY FIBER	9g	VITAMIN C	35%
PROTEIN	16g	VITAMIN A	10%
		IRON	15%

Whole-Wheat Turkey and Veggie
Pita Sandwich

This pita sandwich is a great light lunch option. It travels well, and it has great flavor and a satisfying crunch thanks to all the fresh vegetables.

1 Spread mayonnaise inside halves of pita bread.

2 Fill pita with turkey breast, tomato slices, cucumber slices, and red onion slices.

3 Enjoy immediately.

 Easy

PREP 5 mins

YIELD 1 serving

INGREDIENTS

1 TB. mayonnaise
1 (6½-in; 16.5cm) whole-wheat pita bread, cut in half
2 oz. (55g) deli turkey breast
1 small tomato, sliced
4 slices cucumber
2 slices red onion

To make this sandwich vegetarian, omit the turkey; substitute 2 tablespoons hummus for the mayonnaise; and add ¼ avocado, peeled, pitted, and sliced.

To make this sandwich (or its vegetarian version) gluten free, substitute gluten-free bread, or use Bibb lettuce to make it a lettuce wrap.

NUTRITION PER SERVING			
CALORIES	360	FAT	15g
CARBOHYDRATES	44g	CHOLESTEROL	25mg
SUGARS	3g	SODIUM	970mg
DIETARY FIBER	6g	VITAMIN C	35%
PROTEIN	17g	VITAMIN A	35%
		IRON	15%

Sweet and Salty **Peanut Bars**

These sweet and salty bars are a delicious alternative to store-bought options, thanks to the dried fruit, nuts, and heart-healthy oats.

● ○ ○ ○ **Easy**

PREP 10 mins
COOK 25 to 30 mins

YIELD 12 servings

INGREDIENTS

1 cup dried dates, pitted and finely chopped
¼ cup honey
½ cup creamy peanut butter
1 cup roasted salted peanuts, roughly chopped
1½ cups rolled oats

1 Line a 8×8-inch (20×20cm) baking dish with waxed paper.

2 In a medium bowl, combine dates, honey, peanut butter, peanuts, and rolled oats.

3 Press nut mixture into the bottom of the prepared baking dish, and refrigerate for 25 to 30 minutes.

4 When nut mixture has hardened, remove from the pan and cut into 12 even bars. Store leftovers in a zipper-lock plastic bag.

Make ahead and freeze: Prepare up to step 4, store in an airtight container at room temperature or refrigerate for up to 1 week, or freeze for up to 1 month.

You can make this recipe gluten free by using gluten-free oats.

NUTRITION PER SERVING			
CALORIES	240	FAT	12g
CARBOHYDRATES	27g	CHOLESTEROL	0mg
SUGARS	7g	SODIUM	150mg
DIETARY FIBER	3g	VITAMIN C	2%
PROTEIN	8g	VITAMIN A	0%
		IRON	8%

Tropical Island **Snack Mix**

A good snack mix can help fill you up to keep you "running" at top capacity. This one does just this. Divide this mix into serving sizes, and store in small containers you can keep on you for a quick, healthy snack throughout the day.

1 In a large bowl, toss together almonds, Brazil nuts, hazelnuts, pumpkin seeds, banana chips, pineapple chunks, papaya chunks, coconut chips, dark chocolate chips, and cinnamon until combined.

2 Store in an airtight container for up to 2 weeks.

Make ahead: Store in an airtight container at room temperature for up to 3 days.

 Easy

PREP 5 mins

YIELD 12 servings

INGREDIENTS

¾ cup roasted, salted almonds
½ cup roasted, salted Brazil nuts
¼ cup roasted hazelnuts
¼ cup roasted pumpkin seeds
¼ cup dried banana chips
¼ cup dried pineapple chunks
¼ cup dried papaya chunks
¼ cup coconut chips
¼ cup dark chocolate chips
1 tsp. ground cinnamon

NUTRITION PER SERVING			
CALORIES	200	FAT	16g
CARBOHYDRATES	13g	CHOLESTEROL	0mg
SUGARS	7g	SODIUM	40mg
DIETARY FIBER	4g	VITAMIN C	20%
PROTEIN	5g	VITAMIN A	0%
		IRON	6%

If you have difficulty finding Brazil nuts and hazelnuts, you can replace the almonds, Brazil nuts, and hazelnuts with 1½ cups of your favorite mixed nuts.

Blueberry Madness **Bars**

These bars are a delicious treat, thanks to the sweet fresh blueberries and a satisfyingly crunchy crumb topping.

●●● ○ **Intermediate**

PREP 15 mins
COOK 50 mins

YIELD 12 servings

INGREDIENTS

1½ cups sugar
1 tsp. baking powder
1 cup all-purpose flour
¼ tsp. salt
½ tsp. ground cinnamon
⅓ cup rolled oats
1 cup unsalted butter, diced
1 large egg
3 tsp. cornstarch
4 cups fresh blueberries

1 Preheat the oven to 375°F (190°C). Lightly grease a 9×13-inch (23×33cm) baking pan.

2 In a medium bowl, combine 1 cup sugar, baking powder, all-purpose flour, salt, and cinnamon. Add rolled oats, and stir into flour mixture until evenly distributed.

3 Use a pastry cutter or fork to blend in unsalted butter and egg until dough has a crumbly appearance.

4 Press ¾ of dough mixture into the prepared baking pan.

5 In another medium bowl, stir together remaining ½ cup sugar and cornstarch. Gently fold in blueberries, and pour blueberry mixture over crust.

6 Crumble remaining dough over blueberry layer.

7 Bake for 45 to 50 minutes or until top is lightly golden brown.

8 Cool completely before cutting into 12 bars.

Make ahead and freeze: Prepare up to step 8, store in an airtight container at room temperature for up to 3 days, refrigerate for up to 1 week, or freeze for up to 1 month.

To make these bars gluten free, use gluten-free all-purpose flour. Also, be sure your oats are gluten free.

NUTRITION PER SERVING			
CALORIES	280	FAT	16g
CARBOHYDRATES	34g	CHOLESTEROL	60mg
SUGARS	28g	SODIUM	100mg
DIETARY FIBER	0g	VITAMIN C	0%
PROTEIN	2g	VITAMIN A	10%
		IRON	4%

Coffeecake **Power Muffins**

This portable version of the classic breakfast cake features whole-wheat flour and healthy oils but still keeps that delicious and crunchy crumb topping.

● ● ○ **Intermediate**

PREP 10 mins
COOK about 32 mins

YIELD 12 servings

INGREDIENTS

Crumb topping
⅓ cup granulated sugar
⅓ cup brown sugar, packed
1 tsp. ground cinnamon
¼ tsp. salt
½ cup unsalted butter, melted
1 cup all-purpose flour
½ cup whole-wheat flour
¼ cup rolled oats

Muffin mixture
1 cup all-purpose flour
½ cup whole-wheat flour
½ cup brown sugar, packed
2 tsp. baking powder
1 tsp. ground cinnamon
¼ tsp. baking soda
¼ tsp. salt
¾ cup skim milk
⅓ cup olive oil
2 large eggs

To make this recipe gluten free, substitute gluten-free all-purpose flour.

1 Preheat the oven to 375°F (190°C). Line a 12-cup muffin pan with paper liners or coat with pan spray.

2 *For crumb topping:* in a medium bowl, combine granulated sugar, brown sugar, cinnamon, and salt. Whisk in melted unsalted butter until combined.

3 Add all-purpose flour, whole-wheat flour, and rolled oats, and stir using a spoon or rubber spatula until moist. Spread out mixture on the bottom of the bowl, and set aside.

4 *For muffins:* in a large bowl, stir together all-purpose flour, whole-wheat flour, brown sugar, baking powder, cinnamon, baking soda, and salt until combined.

5 In another medium bowl, whisk together skim milk, olive oil, and eggs.

6 Pour wet ingredients into dry ingredients, and mix with a rubber spatula until moist.

7 Scoop batter evenly among muffin cups, and sprinkle with crumb topping. Gently press crumb topping into batter.

8 Bake for 15 to 17 minutes or until a toothpick inserted into the center comes out clean.

9 Turn out muffins onto a wire rack and allow to cool for at least 10 to 15 minutes before serving. Store leftover muffins in an airtight container.

NUTRITION PER SERVING			
CALORIES	310	FAT	15g
CARBOHYDRATES	41g	CHOLESTEROL	55mg
SUGARS	18g	SODIUM	240mg
DIETARY FIBER	2g	VITAMIN C	0%
PROTEIN	5g	VITAMIN A	6%
		IRON	8%

Bran Raisin **Cookies**

These cookies taste great, are simple to prepare, and will please the entire family.

● ● ● **Intermediate**

PREP 10 mins
COOK 14 mins

YIELD 16 servings

INGREDIENTS

2 cups bran and raisin cereal
1 cup whole-wheat flour
1 cup all-purpose flour
1 tsp. baking soda
¾ cup unsalted butter, softened
⅔ cup granulated sugar
½ cup brown sugar, packed
2 large eggs
½ cup chopped pecans

1 Preheat the oven to 325°F (170°C). Lightly grease a baking sheet with cooking spray.

2 In a medium bowl, crush bran and raisin cereal flakes. Add whole-wheat flour, all-purpose flour, and baking soda, and stir to combine.

3 In a large bowl, beat together unsalted butter, granulated sugar, and brown sugar until light and fluffy.

4 Add eggs, one at a time, and mix well.

5 Gradually stir in dry ingredients, mixing thoroughly after each addition.

6 Gently fold in pecans by hand.

7 Scoop cookies onto the prepared baking sheet using a 2-tablespoon measure or a 2-tablespoon-size cookie scoop.

8 Bake for 12 to 14 minutes or until cookies are lightly browned. Cool cookies on a wire rack for 10 to 12 minutes before storing in an airtight container.

Make ahead and freeze: Prepare dough up to end of step 7 up to 3 days ahead. Freeze after step 7 for up to 2 months.

NUTRITION PER SERVING			
CALORIES	240	FAT	12g
CARBOHYDRATES	33g	CHOLESTEROL	55mg
SUGARS	18g	SODIUM	130mg
DIETARY FIBER	3g	VITAMIN C	0%
PROTEIN	3g	VITAMIN A	6%
		IRON	8%

To keep cookies soft, store them with a slice of bread.

Quick and Easy **Energy Bars**

These energy bars come together so quickly, you'll want to make them all the time. And the recipe is quite versatile. You can change the nuts and fruits to make many different flavor combinations.

1 Line the bottom of an 8×8-inch (20×20cm) baking pan with wax paper.

2 In a food processor fitted with a chopping blade, process cashews, cherries, and dates for 25 to 30 seconds.

3 Scrape down the sides of the bowl, and process for 1 or 2 more minutes or until ingredients form a ball. Press mixture evenly into the bottom of the prepared baking pan.

4 Sprinkle dark chocolate chips over top, and press into fruit and nut mixture.

5 Cover with plastic wrap, and refrigerate overnight.

6 After bars have chilled, cut into 16 bars. Wrap each bar individually with plastic wrap, and store in the refrigerator for up to 3 weeks.

Make ahead and freeze: Prepare up to step 6, store in an airtight container at room temperature or refrigerate for up to 1 week, or freeze for up to 1 month.

● ● ● ● **Easy**

PREP 10 mins

YIELD 8 servings

INGREDIENTS

1 cup cashews
1 cup dried cherries
1 cup dried dates
½ cup dark chocolate chips

NUTRITION PER SERVING			
CALORIES	270	FAT	12g
CARBOHYDRATES	40g	CHOLESTEROL	0mg
SUGARS	15g	SODIUM	80mg
DIETARY FIBER	3g	VITAMIN C	4%
PROTEIN	4g	VITAMIN A	8%
		IRON	6%

You can enjoy these bars chilled for a firmer bite, or let them warm to room temperature for a softer texture.

Orange Ginger **Muffins**

With the sweetness of the oranges and the zing of crystallized ginger (available in the spice aisle of many groceries), these muffins are a tasty treat to have any time of day. And just wait until you smell them while they're baking!

  **Intermediate**

PREP 10 to 15 mins
COOK 18 to 20 mins

YIELD 12 servings

INGREDIENTS

1 cup all-purpose flour
¾ cup whole-wheat flour
1½ tsp. baking powder
1½ tsp. baking soda
½ tsp. salt
1 medium orange
½ cup unsalted butter, softened
¾ cup sugar
1 large egg
½ cup freshly squeezed
    orange juice
¼ cup crystallized ginger,
    finely chopped

For a delicious flavor variation, add ½ cup dried cranberries when folding in the crystallized ginger.

1   Preheat the oven to 375°F (190°C). Line a 12-cup muffin pan with paper liners or lightly grease with pan spray.

2   In a large bowl, combine all-purpose flour, whole-wheat flour, baking powder, baking soda, and salt.

3   Finely grate orange peel into a small bowl until you have 1 or 2 tablespoons zest.

4   Peel and finely chop orange, removing any seeds, and set aside with orange zest.

5   In a large bowl, and using an electric mixer on medium speed, beat together unsalted butter and sugar until light and fluffy. Add egg, and beat until combined.

6   Stir in chopped orange and orange zest, and gradually beat in flour mixture, alternating with orange juice. Fold in crystallized ginger.

7   Divide batter evenly among muffin cups, and bake for 18 to 20 minutes or until a toothpick inserted into center comes out clean.

8   Turn out muffins onto a wire rack, and cool for 10 to 15 minutes. Store leftovers in an airtight container at room temperature, or freeze.

NUTRITION PER SERVING			
CALORIES	240	FAT	8g
CARBOHYDRATES	41g	CHOLESTEROL	40mg
SUGARS	23g	SODIUM	330mg
DIETARY FIBER	4g	VITAMIN C	110%
PROTEIN	4g	VITAMIN A	15%
		IRON	6%

Carb-Loaded Bean and Vegetable **Soup**

This hearty, satisfying soup is full of flavor, with plenty of carbs and protein for fall and winter workouts.

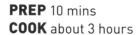
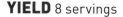

●●● **Easy**

PREP 10 mins
COOK about 3 hours

YIELD 8 servings

INGREDIENTS

2 TB. extra-virgin olive oil

1 medium sweet yellow onion, chopped

½ cup dry white wine

1½ cups dried mixed beans, soaked in water overnight and drained

1 qt. (1l) low-sodium chicken broth

2 qt. (2l) low-sodium beef broth

3 bay leaves

1 (28-oz.; 800g) can whole tomatoes, crushed by hand

2 TB. chopped fresh parsley

2 tsp. chopped fresh thyme

1 tsp. chopped fresh oregano

1 cup uncooked wild rice

4 cups frozen mixed vegetables

½ tsp. salt

¼ tsp. freshly cracked black pepper

1 In a large soup pot over medium-high heat, heat extra-virgin olive oil. Add yellow onion, and cook, stirring occasionally, for 10 to 15 minutes or until onions are a deep golden-brown color.

2 Add white wine to the pot, and deglaze, stirring to remove any browned bits from the bottom of the pan. Cook for about 2 or 3 minutes or until liquid is almost completely absorbed.

3 Add drained mixed beans, chicken broth, beef broth, and bay leaves. Bring to a boil, cover, reduce heat to medium, and simmer for about 2 hours or until beans are almost tender. Skim off and discard any foam on top of soup.

4 Stir in tomatoes, parsley, thyme, oregano, and wild rice, and simmer for about 20 to 30 minutes or until rice and beans are tender.

5 Stir in mixed vegetables, and cook for about 10 minutes or until cooked through. Season with salt and black pepper, and remove bay leaves.

6 Serve immediately.

Make ahead and freeze: Prepare up to the end of step 5 up to 6 days ahead. Freeze in individual containers after step 5 for up to 2 months.

NUTRITION PER SERVING			
CALORIES	360	FAT	6g
CARBOHYDRATES	54g	CHOLESTEROL	0mg
SUGARS	10g	SODIUM	420mg
DIETARY FIBER	6g	VITAMIN C	25%
PROTEIN	19g	VITAMIN A	25%
		IRON	25%

Lentil **Soup**

This is a brothy soup for a cold day. It's perfect to eat right away, or to prepare in a large batch and freeze in individual servings for later.

● ● ● ● **Easy**

PREP 10 mins
COOK 1 hour

YIELD 10 servings

INGREDIENTS

3 qt. (3l) low-sodium chicken broth

3 cups dried lentils, rinsed

2 TB. extra-virgin olive oil

1 large yellow onion, chopped

3 large carrots, peeled and chopped

2 tsp. balsamic vinegar

½ tsp. salt

½ tsp. freshly cracked black pepper

To make this recipe vegetarian, substitute vegetable broth for the chicken broth.

1 In a large pot over high heat, heat chicken broth and lentils. Bring to boil, reduce temperature to low, and simmer for about 1 hour or until lentils are tender. Skim off and discard any foam on top of soup.

2 Meanwhile, in a large sauté pan over medium heat, heat extra-virgin olive oil. Add yellow onion, and cook for about 5 minutes or until softened.

3 Add carrots, and cook for about 5 minutes or until slightly tender. Remove from heat, and set aside.

4 During the last 15 to 20 minutes of lentil cook time, add onions and carrots to lentils. Stir in balsamic vinegar, salt, and black pepper, and continue to cook.

5 Serve hot.

Make ahead and freeze: Prepare up to end of step 3 up to 6 days ahead. Freeze in individual containers after step 3 for up to 2 months.

NUTRITION PER SERVING			
CALORIES	240	FAT	4g
CARBOHYDRATES	37g	CHOLESTEROL	0mg
SUGARS	3g	SODIUM	220mg
DIETARY FIBER	9g	VITAMIN C	4%
PROTEIN	15g	VITAMIN A	70%
		IRON	20%

Maryland Vegetable Crab **Soup**

Fuel up for your workout with this delicious Maryland blue crab soup with veggies—a quick and easy classic from the Chesapeake Bay area.

1 In a large pot over medium-high heat, combine stewed tomatoes with juice, water, mixed vegetables, yellow onion, Old Bay Seasoning, and beef broth. Bring to a boil, reduce heat to medium, and simmer, covered, for 5 to 10 minutes.

2 Stir in blue crabmeat, cover, and simmer for 10 to 15 more minutes.

3 Serve immediately.

Make ahead and freeze: Prepare up to end of step 2 up to 6 days ahead. Freeze in individual containers after step 2 for up to 2 months.

 Easy

PREP 5 mins
COOK about 25 mins

YIELD 10 servings

INGREDIENTS

2 (14.5-oz.; 410g) cans stewed
 tomatoes, with juice

3 cups water

3 cups frozen mixed vegetables

1 small sweet yellow onion, diced

2 TB. Old Bay Seasoning

2 cups low-sodium beef broth

1 lb. (450g) blue crabmeat

NUTRITION PER SERVING			
CALORIES	120	FAT	1g
CARBOHYDRATES	11g	CHOLESTEROL	55mg
SUGARS	5g	SODIUM	450mg
DIETARY FIBER	2g	VITAMIN C	25%
PROTEIN	13g	VITAMIN A	25%
		IRON	6%

If you're having trouble locating Old Bay Seasoning, you can use Creole seasoning—or search online for a suitable spice blend recipe.

Greek Pasta **Salad**

You'll love this easy marinated salad, made with tangy feta cheese, fresh vegetables, and delicious Greek dressing.

 **Easy**

PREP 10 mins + 2 hours
marinate time
COOK 5 to 10 mins

YIELD 8 servings

INGREDIENTS

3 cups tri-colored rotini pasta

2 cups baby spinach leaves

1 cup crumbled feta cheese

1 cup cherry tomatoes, halved

¾ cup canned chickpeas, drained
and rinsed

1 (2.25-oz.; 65g) can sliced black
olives, drained

½ cup bottled Greek dressing

1 In a large pot over medium-high heat, cook tri-colored rotini pasta according to the package directions. Drain cooked pasta, pour into a large bowl, and cool for 5 to 10 minutes.

2 Add spinach leaves, feta cheese, cherry tomatoes, chickpeas, black olives, and Greek dressing, and mix lightly until all ingredients are coated with dressing.

3 Cover salad, and refrigerate for 1 or 2 hours or until cooled.

4 Enjoy chilled.

Make ahead: Refrigerate for 3 to 5 days.

NUTRITION PER SERVING			
CALORIES	310	FAT	13g
CARBOHYDRATES	42g	CHOLESTEROL	15mg
SUGARS	3g	SODIUM	480mg
DIETARY FIBER	5g	VITAMIN C	20%
PROTEIN	11g	VITAMIN A	45%
		IRON	20%

Classic Chef **Salad**

This is an excellent high-protein salad with filling meats and cheeses. It's quick to whip up and perfect to make ahead and take with you.

● ● ● **Easy**

PREP 10 mins

YIELD 2 servings

INGREDIENTS

4 cups mixed salad greens
½ cup ham, sliced
½ cup turkey, sliced
1 small red onion, sliced (¼ cup)
½ cup cherry tomatoes
¼ cup Swiss cheese, sliced
¼ cup cheddar cheese, sliced
2 large hard-boiled eggs, peeled
   and cut in quarters
⅛ cup bacon bits
4 oz. (120ml) salad dressing
   of choice

1 Evenly divide mixed salad greens between two bowls or large plates. Top with ham, turkey, red onion, cherry tomatoes, Swiss cheese, cheddar cheese, hard-boiled egg, and bacon bits.

2 Top with dressing.

3 Enjoy immediately.

Make ahead: Refrigerate mixed greens, chopped eggs, meats, and vegetables in separate containers for quick assembly.

If you're watching your fat intake, you could use reduced-fat cheeses. To lower the sodium, opt for reduced- or low-sodium deli meats, or turkey and ham you've prepared at home.

NUTRITION PER SERVING*			
CALORIES	320	FAT	14g
CARBOHYDRATES	13g	CHOLESTEROL	280mg
SUGARS	5g	SODIUM	1, 540mg
DIETARY FIBER	2g	VITAMIN C	45%
PROTEIN	37g	VITAMIN A	60%
		IRON	10%

*Recipe analyzed without dressing included.

Chickpea **Salad**

This simple marinated salad combines fresh lemon, a little nuttiness from the fresh Parmesan cheese, and delicious fresh herbs with filling chickpeas.

1 In a medium bowl, combine chickpeas, basil, parsley, lemon juice, extra-virgin olive oil, garlic, Parmesan cheese, kosher salt, and black pepper.

2 Serve chilled or at room temperature.

Make ahead: Refrigerate for 3 to 5 days.

 Easy

PREP about 10 mins

YIELD 2 servings

INGREDIENTS

1 (15.5-oz.; 440g) can chickpeas, drained and rinsed

2 TB. chopped fresh basil

2 TB. chopped fresh parsley

2 TB. fresh lemon juice

4 tsp. extra-virgin olive oil

1 clove garlic, chopped finely

⅓ cup freshly grated Parmesan cheese

¼ tsp. kosher salt

¼ tsp. freshly cracked black pepper

To turn this recipe into a tasty hummus, in a food processor, blend chickpeas, lemon juice, extra-virgin olive oil, garlic, Parmesan cheese, kosher salt, and black pepper plus 2 tablespoons tahini paste for 3 to 5 minutes or until smooth. Top with chopped basil and parsley, and serve with pita chips or vegetables.

NUTRITION PER SERVING			
CALORIES	380	FAT	19g
CARBOHYDRATES	32g	CHOLESTEROL	20mg
SUGARS	5g	SODIUM	800mg
DIETARY FIBER	9g	VITAMIN C	15%
PROTEIN	118g	VITAMIN A	2%
		IRON	15%

Sun-Dried Tomato and Feta **Omelet**

This tasty omelet provides a great source of protein before a morning workout.

1 In a small skillet over medium heat, heat extra-virgin olive oil. Add eggs, and cook, swirling eggs with a fork as they set, for 1 or 2 minutes.

2 When eggs are still slightly runny in the middle, scatter sun-dried tomatoes and feta cheese over top, and fold omelet in half. Season with black pepper.

3 Cook for 1 more minute before sliding onto a plate and serving.

● ● ● **Easy**

PREP 5 mins
COOK about 3 mins

YIELD 1 serving

INGREDIENTS

1 tsp. extra-virgin olive oil

2 large eggs, lightly beaten

4 sun-dried tomatoes, roughly chopped

2 TB. crumbled feta cheese

1/8 tsp. freshly cracked black pepper

NUTRITION PER SERVING			
CALORIES	260	FAT	16g
CARBOHYDRATES	11g	CHOLESTEROL	435mg
SUGARS	5g	SODIUM	650mg
DIETARY FIBER	2g	VITAMIN C	8%
PROTEIN	18g	VITAMIN A	20%
		IRON	15%

To boost the protein while keeping the fat down, add ¼ cup diced low-sodium ham for an extra 9 grams protein.

Stuffed Zucchini **Boats**

This summertime dish is packed with protein and great flavor, thanks to the Italian sausage, fresh summer vegetables, and Parmesan cheese.

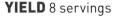 **Intermediate**

PREP 10 to 15 mins
COOK about 40 to 50 mins

YIELD 8 servings

INGREDIENTS

4 large zucchini

1 TB. extra-virgin olive oil

8 oz. (225g) Italian sausage links, casings removed

½ small red onion, finely chopped

1 pt. (470ml) cherry tomatoes, halved

1 tsp. kosher salt

½ tsp. freshly cracked black pepper

⅓ cup panko breadcrumbs

¼ cup freshly grated Parmesan cheese

2 TB. chopped fresh parsley or 1 TB. dried parsley

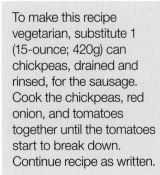

To make this recipe vegetarian, substitute 1 (15-ounce; 420g) can chickpeas, drained and rinsed, for the sausage. Cook the chickpeas, red onion, and tomatoes together until the tomatoes start to break down. Continue recipe as written.

1 Preheat the oven to 350°F (180°C). Lightly grease a baking sheet with cooking spray.

2 In a large, deep skillet over medium-high heat, place zucchini. Cover halfway with water, and bring to a simmer. Reduce heat to low, cover, and cook for 6 to 8 minutes or until tender-crisp. Remove from heat.

3 Drain and dry skillet. Set over medium-high heat, and add extra-virgin olive oil and Italian sausage links. Cook, stirring, for about 4 minutes. Stir in red onion, and cook for about 4 minutes. Add cherry tomatoes, season with kosher salt and black pepper, and cook for 1 minute or until tomatoes start to cook down. Remove from heat.

4 Trim ends off zucchinis and slice in half lengthwise. Scoop out centers, making a boat shape. Chop scooped-out centers and add to sausage mixture. Evenly divide sausage mixture among zucchini shells, and set zucchinis on the baking sheet.

5 In a small bowl, combine panko breadcrumbs, Parmesan cheese, and parsley. Sprinkle over stuffed zucchinis.

6 Bake for about 25 minutes or until topping is golden brown and squash is cooked through. Serve hot.

NUTRITION PER SERVING			
CALORIES	180	FAT	12g
CARBOHYDRATES	8g	CHOLESTEROL	25mg
SUGARS	2g	SODIUM	810mg
DIETARY FIBER	1g	VITAMIN C	15%
PROTEIN	10g	VITAMIN A	10%
		IRON	4%

Whole-Wheat Oatmeal **Pancakes**

Your whole family will love these pancakes, which are a much healthier version than the classic pancake with whole grains and added fiber.

 ● ● ● **Easy**

PREP 5 mins
COOK 5 to 10 mins for
all pancakes

YIELD 3 servings

INGREDIENTS

¾ cup quick-cooking oats
1½ cups plus 2 TB. buttermilk
¾ cup whole-wheat flour
1½ tsp. baking powder
¾ tsp. baking soda
½ tsp. ground cinnamon
⅛ tsp. grated nutmeg
1 large egg, lightly beaten
2 TB. vegetable oil
1½ TB. brown sugar, packed

1 In a medium bowl, combine quick-cooking oats and ¾ cup buttermilk. Set aside to soak for about 10 minutes.

2 Meanwhile, heat a griddle pan over medium heat. Lightly grease with cooking spray.

3 In a large bowl, whisk together whole-wheat flour, baking powder, baking soda, cinnamon, and nutmeg.

4 Stir in egg, vegetable oil, and brown sugar, remaining ¾ cup plus 2 tablespoons buttermilk, as well as oat mixture until just combined.

5 Pour about ¼ cup batter per pancake onto the hot griddle, and cook for about 1 minute or until bubbles appear on surface of pancake and underneath is golden brown. Flip pancake with a spatula, and cook other side for about 30 seconds to 1 minute more.

6 Serve immediately.

Storage: Freeze leftovers, and reheat in a toaster oven.

You can serve these pancakes with your favorite syrup, or top with fresh fruit like bananas, blueberries, or strawberries for different flavors.

NUTRITION PER SERVING			
CALORIES	380	FAT	14g
CARBOHYDRATES	52g	CHOLESTEROL	80mg
SUGARS	14g	SODIUM	760mg
DIETARY FIBER	6g	VITAMIN C	2%
PROTEIN	14g	VITAMIN A	4%
		IRON	15%

Teriyaki Salmon

This sweet and salty salmon dish can be paired with rice and stir-fried vegetables or even served over an Asian-inspired salad.

1 In a small saucepan over low heat, combine sesame oil, orange juice, soy sauce, brown sugar, sesame seeds, ground mustard, ginger, black pepper, and garlic powder. Bring to a simmer, stirring until sugar has dissolved. Set aside ½ cup marinade.

2 Pour remaining marinade into a zipper-lock plastic bag, add salmon steaks, and marinate in the refrigerator for 1 or 2 hours. Drain, and discard marinade.

3 Set top oven rack about 4 inches (10cm) from the heat, and preheat the oven to broil.

4 Place salmon steaks on a baking sheet, place under the broiler, and cook for 5 minutes.

5 Brush salmon with reserved marinade, turn over, and broil for about 5 more minutes or until salmon is cooked through.

6 Remove salmon from the oven, flip over steaks, top with remaining marinade, and cover with aluminum foil. Allow salmon to rest, covered, for 5 to 10 minutes before serving.

Make ahead and freeze: Prepare up to end of step 2 up to 3 days ahead. Freeze after step 2 for up to 2 months.

 Easy

PREP 4 hours
COOK 20 mins

YIELD 4 servings

INGREDIENTS

¼ cup sesame oil

Juice of 1 medium orange (¼ cup)

¼ cup low-sodium soy sauce

2 TB. brown sugar, packed

1 TB. sesame seeds

1 tsp. ground mustard

1 tsp. ground ginger

¼ tsp. freshly cracked black pepper

¼ tsp. garlic powder

4 (4-oz.; 110g) salmon steaks

NUTRITION PER SERVING			
CALORIES	410	FAT	30g
CARBOHYDRATES	10g	CHOLESTEROL	60mg
SUGARS	8g	SODIUM	460mg
DIETARY FIBER	0g	VITAMIN C	8%
PROTEIN	25g	VITAMIN A	2%
		IRON	4%

Power-Packed Cauliflower **Tacos**

Crispy chickpeas and roasted cauliflower offer some tasty calories as well as a few extra carbs and protein in this vegetarian dish.

● ● ◐ **Intermediate**

PREP 2 mins
COOK 1 hour, 5 mins

YIELD 4 servings

INGREDIENTS

1 medium (2-lb.; 1kg) head cauliflower, separated into florets

3 TB. extra-virgin olive oil

1 tsp. kosher salt

1 (15-oz.; 420g) can chickpeas, drained and rinsed

¼ tsp. chili powder

¼ tsp. ground cumin

¼ tsp. dried oregano

½ cup salsa verde

8 (6-in.; 15.25cm) corn tortillas

1 Preheat the oven to 425°F (220°C).

2 Place cauliflower florets in a large bowl. Drizzle with 2 tablespoons extra-virgin olive oil, sprinkle with ½ teaspoon kosher salt, and stir until evenly coated.

3 Arrange cauliflower on a large baking sheet, and bake for 15 minutes. Stir cauliflower, and bake for 15 to 20 more minutes or until cauliflower is browned.

4 Meanwhile, in a small bowl, combine chickpeas, chili powder, cumin, oregano, and remaining ½ teaspoon kosher salt.

5 Spread chickpea mixture in a 9×13-inch (23×33cm) baking pan, and bake for 15 minutes. Stir chickpeas, and bake for 10 to 15 more minutes or until chickpeas are slightly browned and crispy.

6 Spoon about 1 tablespoon salsa verde onto each corn tortilla, and top with about ½ cup roasted cauliflower and 1 tablespoon crispy chickpeas.

7 Serve immediately.

Storage: Refrigerate leftover filling for 3 to 5 days.

For gluten-free tacos, use gluten-free corn tortilla shells.

NUTRITION PER SERVING			
CALORIES	400	FAT	15g
CARBOHYDRATES	56g	CHOLESTEROL	0mg
SUGARS	9g	SODIUM	960mg
DIETARY FIBER	11g	VITAMIN C	190%
PROTEIN	11g	VITAMIN A	4%
		IRON	15%

Three Cheese and Spinach
Stuffed Shells

A great dish for the whole family, these stuffed shells feature fresh wilted spinach, garlic, and three kinds of cheese. They pack a delicious carb and protein punch!

 Intermediate

PREP 10 mins
COOK 40 mins

YIELD 8 servings

INGREDIENTS

24 (8-oz.; 225g) jumbo pasta shells

1½ tsp. extra-virgin olive oil

2 small sweet yellow onions, chopped

2 lb. (1kg) fresh baby spinach, washed

2 cups part-skim ricotta cheese

⅔ cup plain breadcrumbs

½ cup grated Parmesan cheese

¼ cup part-skim mozzarella cheese

¼ tsp. ground nutmeg

¼ tsp. garlic salt

1 tsp. salt

½ tsp. freshly cracked black pepper

1 large egg white, lightly beaten

3 cups prepared marinara sauce

1 Preheat the oven to 375°F (190°C).

2 In a large pot of boiling water over medium-high heat, cook pasta shells, stirring often, for about 15 minutes. Drain, rinse under cool water, and set aside.

3 In a large skillet over medium-high heat, heat extra-virgin olive oil. Add sweet yellow onions, and cook, stirring occasionally, for about 3 minutes or until softened.

4 Add baby spinach in batches, and toss until wilted. Drain spinach in a colander and press out excess liquid. Set aside.

5 In a large bowl, combine ricotta cheese, breadcrumbs, ¼ cup Parmesan cheese, mozzarella cheese, and nutmeg. Add spinach, garlic salt, salt, and black pepper, and stir in egg white. Stuff each pasta shell with 2 tablespoons cheese mixture.

6 Spread 1 cup marinara sauce in the bottom of a 9×13-inch (23×33cm) baking dish. Add stuffed shells in a single layer, top with remaining 2 cups marinara sauce, and sprinkle with remaining ¼ cup Parmesan cheese. Bake for about 30 minutes. Cool for 5 to 10 minutes before serving.

NUTRITION PER SERVING			
CALORIES	350	FAT	6g
CARBOHYDRATES	55g	CHOLESTEROL	15mg
SUGARS	5g	SODIUM	1,210mg
DIETARY FIBER	9g	VITAMIN C	30%
PROTEIN	21g	VITAMIN A	90%
		IRON	30%

Shrimp and Spinach **Pasta**

This vibrant dish combines fresh spinach and succulent shrimp with the flavors of lemon, basil, and Parmesan cheese.

1 In a large pot over medium-high heat, cook tri-colored rotini pasta according to the package directions. Ladle 1 cup pasta water into a small bowl, and set aside. Drain pasta, return to the pot, cover, and set aside.

2 Meanwhile, in a large skillet over medium-high heat, heat extra-virgin olive oil. Add shrimp and garlic, and cook, stirring occasionally, for about 2 minutes.

3 Add tomatoes with juice, ⅛ cup basil, lemon juice, and lemon zest, and sauté for about 3 minutes or until shrimp are cooked through.

4 Add baby spinach to hot pasta, and toss until spinach wilts. Add shrimp mixture, and toss to combine. Add reserved pasta water, and stir in Parmesan cheese, salt, black pepper, and remaining ⅛ cup basil.

5 Serve immediately.

● ● ● **Easy**

PREP 10 mins
COOK about 15 mins

YIELD 4 servings

INGREDIENTS

12 oz. (340g) tri-colored rotini pasta

2 TB. extra-virgin olive oil

1 lb. (450g) raw shrimp (16 to 20 count), peeled and deveined

3 cloves garlic, minced

1 (15-oz.; 420g) can diced tomatoes, with juice

¼ cup chopped fresh basil

3 TB. fresh lemon juice

2 tsp. lemon zest

½ lb. (225g) fresh baby spinach, washed

¼ cup grated Parmesan cheese

1 tsp. salt

½ tsp. freshly cracked black pepper

To make this recipe vegetarian, use 1 (15-ounce; 420g) can chickpeas, drained and rinsed, instead of the shrimp.

To make this recipe gluten free, use gluten-free pasta.

NUTRITION PER SERVING

CALORIES	540	FAT	11g
CARBOHYDRATES	76g	CHOLESTEROL	175mg
SUGARS	6g	SODIUM	1,240mg
DIETARY FIBER	6g	VITAMIN C	60%
PROTEIN	39g	VITAMIN A	60%
		IRON	35%

Beef, Broccoli, and Yam **Stir-Fry**

This super stir-fry is loaded with lean protein and yams, which are a great source of fiber and vitamins.

● ● ● **Easy**

PREP 15 mins
COOK about 10 mins

YIELD 4 servings

INGREDIENTS

¼ cup water

1 TB. brown sugar, packed

3 TB. oyster sauce

1 lb. (450g) flank steak, cut into ¼×½-in. (.5×1.25cm) slices

½ tsp. salt

½ tsp. freshly cracked black pepper

1½ TB. cornstarch

2½ TB. sesame oil

4 cups broccoli florets

1 (8-oz.; 225g) yam, cut into ⅓-in. (.75cm) slices

2 tsp. fresh ginger, peeled and finely chopped

¼ tsp. crushed red pepper flakes

1 In small bowl, combine water, brown sugar, and oyster sauce until sugar dissolves. Set sauce aside.

2 Place flank steak in a large bowl. Sprinkle with salt, black pepper, and cornstarch, and toss to coat.

3 In a wok or a large skillet over high heat, heat 1½ tablespoons sesame oil. Add beef mixture, and stir-fry for about 3 minutes or until no longer pink outside. Transfer beef mixture to medium bowl.

4 Return the skillet to heat, and add remaining 1 tablespoon sesame oil. Add broccoli florets, yam, and ginger, and toss to coat.

5 Add crushed red pepper flakes to the skillet along with sauce. Cover, reduce heat to medium-high, and cook for about 5 minutes or until vegetables are just tender.

6 Add beef mixture to the skillet, and toss to coat beef for about 1 minute. Serve hot.

Storage: Refrigerate leftovers for 3 to 5 days.

Feel free to use different protein sources in this recipe, like chicken or shrimp. And if you can't find oyster sauce, substitute soy sauce.

NUTRITION PER SERVING			
CALORIES	390	FAT	19g
CARBOHYDRATES	16g	CHOLESTEROL	60mg
SUGARS	4g	SODIUM	740mg
DIETARY FIBER	5g	VITAMIN C	70%
PROTEIN	33g	VITAMIN A	2%
		IRON	15%

Strawberry Shortcake **Milkshakes**

With plenty of fast-acting carbs and 17 grams of protein per serving, this is a great power smoothie!

1 In a blender, blend vanilla Greek yogurt, skim milk, strawberries, rolled oats, sugar, and vanilla extract for about 3 minutes or until smooth.

2 Serve immediately.

Storage: Refrigerate leftovers in a sealed cup, and stir when ready to eat.

 Easy

PREP 5 mins

YIELD 3 servings

INGREDIENTS

2 cups vanilla Greek yogurt
2 cups skim milk
2 cups fresh or frozen strawberries
¼ cup rolled oats
4 TB. sugar
1 tsp. vanilla extract

NUTRITION PER SERVING			
CALORIES	420	FAT	17g
CARBOHYDRATES	51g	CHOLESTEROL	30mg
SUGARS	30g	SODIUM	170mg
DIETARY FIBER	6g	VITAMIN C	60%
PROTEIN	17g	VITAMIN A	20%
		IRON	4%

Slow Cooker **Rice Pudding**

This quick and easy old-fashioned rice pudding is packed full of carbs to keep your body energized. It's perfect served warm for winter sports or chilled during summer events.

● ● ● **Easy**

PREP 5 mins
COOK 2½ to 3 hours

YIELD 6 servings

INGREDIENTS

¾ cup long-grain white rice
½ cup raisins
3 cups 2% milk
1 cup sugar
¾ tsp. ground cinnamon
⅛ tsp. salt
¼ cup unsalted butter, melted

1 Lightly greased 4-quart (4l) slow cooker with cooking spray.

2 In a colander, rinse long-grain white rice thoroughly under cold water.

3 Pour rice into the slow cooker. Add raisins, 2% milk, sugar, cinnamon, and salt, and stir to combine.

4 Pour unsalted butter over rice mixture and stir to combine. Cover, and cook on high for 2½ to 3 hours or until rice has absorbed all liquids.

5 Serve warm or chilled.

Storage: Refrigerate leftovers for 3 to 5 days.

To add a bit more carbs to this recipe, stir in ¾ cup golden raisins, dried cherries, or chopped dried apricots when you add the butter.

NUTRITION PER SERVING			
CALORIES	400	FAT	10g
CARBOHYDRATES	90g	CHOLESTEROL	30mg
SUGARS	51g	SODIUM	130mg
DIETARY FIBER	1g	VITAMIN C	2%
PROTEIN	7g	VITAMIN A	10%
		IRON	8%

Strawberries and Cream **Ice Pops**

This is a delicious, summery treat, perfect for keeping cool and hydrated during your workout, thanks to delicious fresh strawberries and creamy Greek yogurt.

1   In a medium bowl, combine strawberries, sugar, and vanilla extract. Set aside for about 15 to 20 minutes.

2   In a blender, purée strawberry mixture and vanilla Greek yogurt until smooth.

3   Evenly divide mixture among 6 ice pop molds, and freeze for about 4 hours or until firm.

Storage: Freeze leftovers for up to 1 week.

● ○ ○ **Easy**

PREP 20 mins + 4 hours freeze time

YIELD 6 servings

INGREDIENTS

2 cups fresh strawberries, hulled and sliced

1/3 cup sugar

2 tsp. vanilla extract

1 cup vanilla Greek yogurt

NUTRITION PER SERVING			
CALORIES	120	FAT	4g
CARBOHYDRATES	17g	CHOLESTEROL	5mg
SUGARS	15g	SODIUM	10mg
DIETARY FIBER	1g	VITAMIN C	50%
PROTEIN	3g	VITAMIN A	0%
		IRON	2%

If sugar isn't your preferred sweetener, you can use 1/4 cup agave nectar or honey instead.

Blueberry Orange **Parfaits**

Whip up these tasty parfaits, made with fresh blueberries and sweet oranges, any time you need a little extra protein and carbs.

 Easy

PREP 15 mins

YIELD 4 servings

INGREDIENTS

½ tsp. orange zest

2 cups vanilla Greek yogurt

2 cups fresh blueberries

2 cups orange segments (about 2 large oranges)

1 cup granola cereal

1 In a small bowl, combine orange zest and vanilla Greek yogurt.

2 Spoon ¼ cup blueberries into 4 parfait or tall glasses, followed by about 2½ tablespoons yogurt mixture and ¼ cup orange segments each. Repeat layers with remaining blueberries, yogurt mixture, and orange segments.

3 Sprinkle each serving with ¼ cup granola cereal.

4 Serve immediately.

Make ahead: Refrigerate prepared fruit and yogurt for quick assembly.

Not a fan of blueberries? Substitute the same amount of fresh blackberries or raspberries instead.

NUTRITION PER SERVING			
CALORIES	310	FAT	14g
CARBOHYDRATES	36g	CHOLESTEROL	20mg
SUGARS	23g	SODIUM	45mg
DIETARY FIBER	6g	VITAMIN C	100%
PROTEIN	11g	VITAMIN A	6%
		IRON	4%

Recipes for
Competition

During intense competition, it's important to keep your energy up and maintain proper hydration. In Part 3, we give you a number of nutritionally dense foods you can take on the go, including homemade competition sports drinks, precompetition smoothies, and more delicious and easy-to-prepare competition portables.

Does your competition take place over the course of a whole day, or does it last even longer than a day? Either way, we have you covered with precompetition soups, salads, entrées, and desserts geared toward refueling your body and elevating your energy level.

Staying fueled during a competition has never been easier—nor healthier—with the delicious precompetition and competition recipes that follow.

Mango **Cooler**

Refreshing and delicious, this tropical cooler is just what your body needs to keep you pushing through your workout.

 Easy

PREP 2 mins

YIELD 1 serving

INGREDIENTS

¾ cup mango nectar

1½ cups water

1 TB. sugar

⅛ tsp. salt

1 In a large glass, combine mango nectar, water, sugar, and salt.

2 Drink over ice.

NUTRITION PER SERVING			
CALORIES	120	FAT	0g
CARBOHYDRATES	31g	CHOLESTEROL	0mg
SUGARS	30g	SODIUM	310mg
DIETARY FIBER	0g	VITAMIN C	15%
PROTEIN	0g	VITAMIN A	8%
		IRON	4%

Cranberry **Limeade**

Cranberry and lime juices combine with the sweetness of fresh orange juice in this bubbly, thirst-quenching beverage.

 Easy

PREP 5 mins

YIELD 1 serving

INGREDIENTS

1 TB. Rose's lime juice

⅛ cup fresh orange juice

½ cup cranberry juice

¾ cup club soda

⅛ tsp. salt

1 In a water bottle, combine Rose's lime juice, orange juice, cranberry juice, club soda, and salt.

2 Consume chilled or over ice.

NUTRITION PER SERVING			
CALORIES	130	FAT	0g
CARBOHYDRATES	32g	CHOLESTEROL	0mg
SUGARS	29g	SODIUM	290mg
DIETARY FIBER	0g	VITAMIN C	90%
PROTEIN	0g	VITAMIN A	0%
		IRON	0%

Mango Cooler

Cranberry Limeade

Grapefruit Fizz

Pineapple
Ginger Sipper

Grapefruit **Fizz**

Grapefruits are full of vitamins and minerals, some of which have even been shown to help fight cancer and various diseases. This fizzy drink is bursting with tangy and tart grapefruit flavor, with a hint of sweetness from a splash of grenadine.

  Easy

PREP 2 mins

YIELD 1 serving

INGREDIENTS

Juice of 1½ large grapefruits (¾ cup)

1½ cups club soda

1 TB. grenadine

⅛ tsp. salt

1   In a large glass, combine grapefruit juice, club soda, grenadine, and salt.

2   Drink over ice.

NUTRITION PER SERVING			
CALORIES	140	FAT	0g
CARBOHYDRATES	35g	CHOLESTEROL	0mg
SUGARS	30g	SODIUM	300mg
DIETARY FIBER	0g	VITAMIN C	0%
PROTEIN	0g	VITAMIN A	0%
		IRON	0%

Pineapple Ginger **Sipper**

This sipper is sweet due to delicious pineapple juice and a little zesty thanks to the crystallized ginger.

  Easy

PREP 3 mins

YIELD 1 serving

INGREDIENTS

1¾ cups pineapple juice

½ cup water

1 large piece crystallized ginger, roughly chopped

⅛ tsp. salt

1   In a large glass, combine pineapple juice, water, crystallized ginger, and salt.

2   Drink over ice.

NUTRITION PER SERVING			
CALORIES	230	FAT	0g
CARBOHYDRATES	56g	CHOLESTEROL	0mg
SUGARS	54g	SODIUM	300mg
DIETARY FIBER	0g	VITAMIN C	35%
PROTEIN	0g	VITAMIN A	4%
		IRON	4%

Sparkling Apple Cinnamon
Refresher

This sparkling power drink tastes just like fall, with delicious apple cider and a hint of cinnamon.

 ● ● ● **Easy**

PREP 5 mins

YIELD 3 servings

INGREDIENTS

¼ cup freshly squeezed orange juice (about 2 medium oranges)

2 cups club soda

1½ tsp. sugar

1 (25-oz.; 750ml) bottle sparkling apple cider

½ tsp. ground cinnamon

1 In a water jug, combine orange juice, club soda, sugar, sparkling apple cider, and cinnamon.

2 Consume chilled or over ice.

NUTRITION PER SERVING			
CALORIES	70	FAT	0g
CARBOHYDRATES	18g	CHOLESTEROL	0mg
SUGARS	16g	SODIUM	15mg
DIETARY FIBER	0g	VITAMIN C	0%
PROTEIN	0g	VITAMIN A	0%
		IRON	0%

Creamy Orange and Carrot **Smoothie**

You'll love this sweet orange and zesty ginger smoothie full of vitamins and minerals. It provides an amazing amount of beta-carotene for eye and skin health.

 ● ● ● **Easy**

PREP 3 mins

YIELD 1 serving

INGREDIENTS

¼ cup frozen orange juice concentrate

1 medium carrot, chopped

1 large piece crystallized ginger, roughly chopped

¼ cup 2% milk

¾ cup ice cubes

1 In a blender, combine orange juice concentrate, carrot, crystallized ginger, 2% milk, and ice cubes for about 1 or 2 minutes or until smooth.

2 Drink immediately.

NUTRITION PER SERVING			
CALORIES	190	FAT	1.5g
CARBOHYDRATES	40g	CHOLESTEROL	5mg
SUGARS	34g	SODIUM	110mg
DIETARY FIBER	3g	VITAMIN C	140%
PROTEIN	4g	VITAMIN A	340%
		IRON	2%

Lean, Green, Broccoli **Smoothie**

Broccoli is an unexpected ingredient in a smoothie, and for some, it might not be a favorite option. However, this delicious smoothie is sweet and hides the broccoli flavor well.

 ● ● ● **Easy**

PREP 5 mins

YIELD 2 servings

INGREDIENTS

1½ cups honeydew melon, peeled, seeded, and cubed

1½ cups ice cubes

2 kiwi, peeled

½ medium cucumber, peeled, seeded, and chopped

¼ cup fresh broccoli florets

5 to 10 fresh mint leaves

1 In a blender, combine honeydew melon, ice cubes, kiwi, cucumber, broccoli florets, and mint leaves for about 2 or 3 minutes or until completely combined.

2 Drink immediately.

NUTRITION PER SERVING			
CALORIES	210	FAT	1.5g
CARBOHYDRATES	49g	CHOLESTEROL	0mg
SUGARS	37g	SODIUM	60mg
DIETARY FIBER	8g	VITAMIN C	360%
PROTEIN	4g	VITAMIN A	20%
		IRON	8%

Creamy Orange and
Carrot Smoothie

Lean, Green, Broccoli
Smoothie

Banana Orange
Sunrise Smoothie

Mixed Berry
Blenderita
Smoothie

Banana Orange
Sunrise Smoothie

This simple and delicious smoothie is packed with nutrients and electrolytes to fuel your body.

 Easy

PREP 5 mins

YIELD 1 serving

INGREDIENTS

½ cup 2% milk
2 oz. (60ml) vanilla Greek yogurt
2 tsp. sugar
1 medium orange, peeled and segmented
½ medium banana, peeled and sliced
¾ cup ice cubes

1   In a blender, combine 2% milk, Greek yogurt, sugar, orange segments, banana, and ice cubes for about 1 minute or until smooth.

2   Drink immediately.

NUTRITION PER SERVING

CALORIES	270	FAT	8g
CARBOHYDRATES	42g	CHOLESTEROL	20mg
SUGARS	32g	SODIUM	75mg
DIETARY FIBER	5g	VITAMIN C	130%
PROTEIN	10g	VITAMIN A	10%
		IRON	2%

Mixed Berry
Blenderita Smoothie

This creamy, delicious smoothie is a good source of carbs and protein for your competition days. It's also a great source of vitamin C to protect your cells from harmful free radicals—a by-product of exercising.

 Easy

PREP 5 mins

YIELD 1 serving

INGREDIENTS

½ cup 2% milk
2 oz. (60ml) vanilla Greek yogurt
Juice of 1 orange (¼ cup)
Juice of 2 medium limes (¼ cup)
1 cup frozen mixed berries

1   In a blender, combine 2% milk, Greek yogurt, orange juice, lime juice, and mixed berries for about 1 minute or until smooth.

2   Drink immediately.

NUTRITION PER SERVING

CALORIES	280	FAT	8g
CARBOHYDRATES	41g	CHOLESTEROL	20mg
SUGARS	25g	SODIUM	95mg
DIETARY FIBER	9g	VITAMIN C	70%
PROTEIN	11g	VITAMIN A	15%
		IRON	6%

Peaches and Cream
Smoothie

This thick and creamy smoothie is a terrific source of protein, providing 16 grams per serving to help build your muscles without the use of any protein powders.

 Easy

PREP 5 to 10 mins

YIELD 1 serving

INGREDIENTS

½ cup 2% milk
2 oz. (60ml) vanilla Greek yogurt
¼ cup 1% fat cottage cheese
2 tsp. sugar
¼ cup freshly squeezed orange juice
   (about 2 medium oranges)
¾ cup frozen peaches

1 In a blender, blend 2% milk, vanilla Greek yogurt, cottage cheese, sugar, orange juice, and peaches for about 1 minute or until smooth.

2 Drink immediately.

NUTRITION PER SERVING			
CALORIES	280	FAT	9g
CARBOHYDRATES	35g	CHOLESTEROL	20mg
SUGARS	34g	SODIUM	300mg
DIETARY FIBER	2g	VITAMIN C	160%
PROTEIN	16g	VITAMIN A	10%
		IRON	2%

Green Monster
Smoothie

This is a great green smoothie full of vitamins and minerals to replenish what your body uses during a strenuous workout. Don't be intimidated by the color; you're going to love it!

 Easy

PREP 5 mins

YIELD 1 serving

INGREDIENTS

½ cup 2% milk
½ cup vanilla Greek yogurt
1 small banana, peeled, frozen, and sliced
2 TB. creamy peanut butter
2 cups fresh spinach
1 cup ice cubes

1 In a blender, blend 2% milk, vanilla Greek yogurt, banana, peanut butter, spinach, and ice cubes until smooth.

2 Drink immediately.

NUTRITION PER SERVING			
CALORIES	250	FAT	15g
CARBOHYDRATES	22g	CHOLESTEROL	15mg
SUGARS	12g	SODIUM	160mg
DIETARY FIBER	3g	VITAMIN C	15%
PROTEIN	11g	VITAMIN A	20%
		IRON	6%

Peaches and Cream
Smoothie

Green Monster
Smoothie

Never-Leave-Home-Without-It
Trail Mix

You can make and take this simple and easy trail mix anywhere for a quick snack.

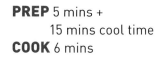

● ● ● ● **Easy**

PREP 5 mins +
            15 mins cool time
COOK 6 mins

YIELD 10 servings

INGREDIENTS

4 cups toasted wheat cereal

½ cup shredded coconut

½ cup dried banana chips

⅔ cup dried tropical fruit (mango, papaya, etc.)

⅓ cup golden raisins

⅓ cup macadamia nuts or cashews

1½ TB. unsalted butter

2 TB. brown sugar, packed

2 TB. frozen pineapple or orange juice concentrate, thawed

1 In a large microwave-safe bowl, combine toasted wheat cereal, coconut, banana chips, tropical fruit, golden raisins, and macadamia nuts. Set aside.

2 In a microwave-safe measuring cup, microwave unsalted butter, uncovered, on high for about 30 seconds or until melted.

3 Stir brown sugar and pineapple juice concentrate into melted butter, and microwave, uncovered, on high for about 30 more seconds or until hot. Stir to combine, pour over cereal mixture, and stir until evenly coated.

4 Microwave, uncovered, on high for 3 to 5 more minutes (times may vary depending on microwave), stirring every 2 minutes as needed until mixture begins to lightly brown.

5 Spread trail mix on waxed paper or aluminum foil to cool for about 10 to 15 minutes.

Storage: Keep in an airtight container for up to 2 days.

This trail mix snack is low in saturated fat and a good source of iron and fiber. To make it gluten free, use rice cereal.

NUTRITION PER SERVING			
CALORIES	260	FAT	8g
CARBOHYDRATES	43g	CHOLESTEROL	0mg
SUGARS	21g	SODIUM	230mg
DIETARY FIBER	4g	VITAMIN C	15%
PROTEIN	4g	VITAMIN A	8%
		IRON	45%

Snack Mix **Cereal Bars**

These bars are a power-packed twist on the classic crispy rice cereal treat with added protein from the peanuts and peanut butter.

1 Lightly grease a 9×13-inch (23×33cm) baking pan with cooking spray.

2 In a large microwave-safe bowl, microwave unsalted butter, uncovered, on high for about 45 seconds or until melted.

3 Add marshmallows, toss to coat, and microwave 1 to 1½ minutes.

4 Add peanut butter, and stir until marshmallows are completely melted and mixture is well blended.

5 Add crispy cereal squares, mini pretzels, peanuts, and mini candy-coated chocolate pieces, and mix well.

6 Using wax paper or a spatula sprayed with cooking spray, press mixture evenly into the prepared baking dish. Set aside to cool for 15 minutes before cutting into 6 rows by 3 rows.

Make ahead and freeze: Prepare up to step 6, store in an airtight container at room temperature or refrigerate for up to 1 week, or freeze for up to 1 month.

● ● ● ● **Easy**

PREP 5 mins
COOK about 3 mins

YIELD 18 servings

INGREDIENTS

¼ cup unsalted butter

1 (10-oz.; 285g) bag large marshmallows

½ cup creamy peanut butter

6 cups crispy wheat cereal squares

1 cup mini pretzels

1 cup dry-roasted, unsalted peanuts

½ cup mini candy-coated chocolate pieces

NUTRITION PER SERVING			
CALORIES	290	FAT	12g
CARBOHYDRATES	41g	CHOLESTEROL	10mg
SUGARS	17g	SODIUM	290mg
DIETARY FIBER	3g	VITAMIN C	4%
PROTEIN	7g	VITAMIN A	6%
		IRON	35%

To make this recipe gluten free, use rice cereal and substitute 1 more cup rice cereal or gluten-free pretzels for the mini pretzels.

Country **Frittata**

For a hearty breakfast dish with ham, potato, and cheddar cheese to get your competition day started, you can't beat this frittata.

 Easy

PREP 5 mins
COOK about 20 mins

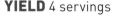

YIELD 4 servings

INGREDIENTS

2 TB. extra-virgin olive oil

1 lb. cooked Idaho potatoes, diced small

¼ cup ham, diced

¼ tsp. garlic, minced

8 large eggs

1 tsp. salt

½ tsp. freshly cracked black pepper

¼ cup grated sharp cheddar cheese

1 Preheat the oven to 350°F (180°C).

2 In a 12-inch (30.5cm) nonstick skillet with an ovenproof handle over medium-high heat, heat extra-virgin olive oil. Add Idaho potatoes, ham, and garlic, and sauté for about 5 minutes or until lightly browned.

3 In a medium bowl, whisk eggs with salt and black pepper. Pour eggs over potato mixture, reduce heat to medium-low, and cook, using a rubber spatula to occasionally scrape around edges of frittata as it cooks, for about 5 to 10 minutes.

4 When eggs are nearly set, sprinkle sharp cheddar cheese over top, and place in the oven for 3 to 5 minutes or until eggs are evenly set and slightly golden.

5 Serve hot.

Storage: Refrigerate leftovers for 3 to 5 days.

For a vegetarian version, omit the ham and add any number of vegetables as a substitute, such as a handful of baby spinach and some diced tomatoes or diced bell peppers.

NUTRITION PER SERVING			
CALORIES	330	FAT	18g
CARBOHYDRATES	25g	CHOLESTEROL	440mg
SUGARS	1g	SODIUM	780mg
DIETARY FIBER	2g	VITAMIN C	15%
PROTEIN	18g	VITAMIN A	15%
		IRON	10%

Baked Egg and Tomato **Cups**

For a quick and easy breakfast or an on-the-go treat with a good bit of protein, these breakfast cups are just what you need.

1 Preheat the oven to 450°F (230°C).

2 Cut roma tomatoes in half and remove the seeds. Slice a small sliver off bottom of each tomato half so it stands up like a cup, and place in a baking pan.

3 Crack eggs and gently place 1 egg inside each tomato cup. Season egg with black pepper, and sprinkle with Gruyère cheese.

4 Bake for 8 to 10 minutes or until eggs are cooked through.

5 Serve hot, or allow to cool and take on the road chilled.

Make ahead: Prepare up to step 4, and refrigerate for up to 5 days.

● ○ ○ **Easy**

PREP 8 mins
COOK 8 to 10 mins

YIELD 4 servings

INGREDIENTS

4 large roma tomatoes
8 small eggs
½ tsp. freshly cracked black pepper
½ cup shredded Gruyère cheese

NUTRITION PER SERVING			
CALORIES	180	FAT	12g
CARBOHYDRATES	4g	CHOLESTEROL	335mg
SUGARS	3g	SODIUM	160mg
DIETARY FIBER	1g	VITAMIN C	20%
PROTEIN	14g	VITAMIN A	25%
		IRON	10%

If you can't find large-enough roma tomatoes to hold your eggs, use small vine-ripe tomatoes instead.

Quickie Breakfast **Burrito**

You can have this super-simple breakfast burrito ready in minutes. Now you no longer have any excuses to skip breakfast on a busy competition day!

● ○ ○ **Easy**

PREP 2 mins
COOK 1 min

YIELD 1 serving

INGREDIENTS

1 (6-in.; 15.25cm) flour tortilla
1 large egg
1 TB. shredded cheddar cheese
1 TB. salsa
¼ tsp. freshly cracked black
   pepper

1 Line a 2-cup microwave-safe cereal bowl with a paper towel. Press flour tortilla into the bowl, break egg into center of tortilla, and beat egg gently with a fork.

2 Microwave on high for 30 seconds, stir, and microwave for about 15 to 30 more seconds or until egg is almost set.

3 Transfer tortilla and paper towel liner from the bowl to a flat surface. Top egg with cheddar cheese, salsa, and black pepper, and wrap egg with tortilla.

4 Enjoy immediately.

To make this recipe gluten free, use a gluten-free corn tortilla.

NU TRITION PER SERVING			
CALORIES	180	FAT	7g
CARBOHYDRATES	18g	CHOLESTEROL	215mg
SUGARS	1g	SODIUM	370mg
DIETARY FIBER	1g	VITAMIN C	2%
PROTEIN	10g	VITAMIN A	8%
		IRON	10%

Low-Fat Banana **Bread**

You'll love this update to the classic banana bread recipe with lower fat.

 Easy

PREP 10 mins
COOK about 1 hour

YIELD 16 servings

INGREDIENTS

2 large eggs
⅔ cup sugar
2 very ripe bananas, peeled and
   mashed
¼ cup cinnamon applesauce
⅓ cup 2% milk
1 TB. vegetable oil
1 TB. vanilla extract
1¾ cups all-purpose flour
2 tsp. baking powder
½ tsp. baking soda
½ tsp. salt
⅓ cup chopped walnuts

1 Preheat the oven to 325°F (170°C). Lightly grease 2 (9×4-inch; 23×10cm) bread pans with cooking spray, dust with flour, and shake out excess flour.

2 In a large bowl, beat eggs and sugar for about 5 minutes or until light and fluffy.

3 Using a rubber spatula, beat in bananas, cinnamon applesauce, 2% milk, vegetable oil, and vanilla extract.

4 In a separate large bowl, sift together all-purpose flour, baking powder, baking soda, and salt. Stir flour mixture into banana mixture, mixing just until blended.

5 Fold in walnuts, and evenly divide batter between the prepared pans.

6 Bake for about 1 hour or until golden and a toothpick inserted into center of each loaf comes out clean.

7 Turn out bread onto a wire rack, and cool.

Make ahead and freeze: Prepare up to end of step 5 up to 3 days ahead. Freeze, sliced or whole, at end of step 7 for up to 2 months.

NUTRITION PER SERVING			
CALORIES	110	FAT	3g
CARBOHYDRATES	20g	CHOLESTEROL	25mg
SUGARS	10g	SODIUM	190mg
DIETARY FIBER	0g	VITAMIN C	0%
PROTEIN	3g	VITAMIN A	0%
		IRON	4%

Turkey and Scallion **Wraps**

These wraps are easy to make and are a great treat to sneak in a good amount of carbs and protein without packing on a ton of calories.

● ● ○ ○　**Easy**

PREP 5 mins

YIELD 4 servings

INGREDIENTS

2 TB. reduced-fat mayonnaise

2 TB. pesto

¾ cup mixed greens

8.8 oz. (250g) deli turkey (number of slices will vary with thickness of slices)

6 scallions, sliced

16 slices cucumber

4 (6-in.; 15.25cm) flour tortillas

1 In a small bowl, combine mayonnaise and pesto.

2 Evenly divide mixed greens, turkey, scallions, and cucumber slices among tortillas.

3 Drizzle pesto dressing over top, and roll tortillas.

4 Enjoy immediately.

Make ahead: Prepare pesto mayo and slice vegetables up to 3 days ahead, and refrigerate for quick assembly.

To make this recipe gluten free, use gluten-free corn tortillas.

NUTRITION PER SERVING			
CALORIES	240	FAT	10g
CARBOHYDRATES	22g	CHOLESTEROL	30mg
SUGARS	3g	SODIUM	860mg
DIETARY FIBER	2g	VITAMIN C	10%
PROTEIN	15g	VITAMIN A	15%
		IRON	10%

Chickpea, Tomato, and Pasta **Soup**

This is a very light and easy vegetarian soup that contains a decent amount of protein and plenty of carbs.

1   In a large pot over medium-high heat, bring vegetable broth to a boil. Add elbow macaroni, and cook for 8 to 10 minutes or until al dente.

2   Meanwhile, in a small skillet over medium heat, heat extra-virgin olive oil. Add sweet yellow onion and garlic, and sauté for 5 to 10 minutes or until translucent.

3   Transfer onions and garlic to pasta pot, and add chickpeas, tomatoes, basil, thyme, salt, and black pepper. Stir and heat through.

4   Serve hot.

Make ahead and freeze: Prepare up to end of step 3 up to 6 days ahead. Freeze in individual containers after step 3 for up to 2 months.

● ● ● ●   **Easy**

PREP 15 mins
COOK about 20 mins

YIELD 4 servings

INGREDIENTS

3 (14.5-oz.; 410g) cans low-sodium vegetable broth

¾ cup elbow macaroni

1 TB. extra-virgin olive oil

1 medium sweet yellow onion, chopped

2 cloves garlic, minced

1 (15-oz.; 420g) can chickpeas, drained and rinsed

1 (28-oz.; 800g) can diced tomatoes, with juice

½ tsp. dried basil

½ tsp. dried thyme

¼ tsp. salt

½ tsp. freshly cracked black pepper

NUTRITION PER SERVING			
CALORIES	260	FAT	5g
CARBOHYDRATES	44g	CHOLESTEROL	0mg
SUGARS	12g	SODIUM	760mg
DIETARY FIBER	8g	VITAMIN C	60%
PROTEIN	10g	VITAMIN A	25%
		IRON	20%

Easy Minestrone **Soup**

This vegetable-rich vegetarian soup will warm you up and keep you moving.

● ● ● ● **Easy**

PREP 15 mins
COOK about 40 mins

YIELD 4 servings

INGREDIENTS

2 TB. extra-virgin olive oil

1 small white onion, chopped

3 cloves garlic, minced

2 medium celery stalks, rinsed and diced

1 medium zucchini, diced

1 cup fresh green beans, cut in ½-in. (1.25cm) pieces

1 medium carrot, peeled and diced

2 (14-oz.; 400g) cans diced tomatoes, with juice

4 cups reduced-sodium vegetable broth

2 cups water

1 (14-oz.; 400g) can cannellini beans, rinsed and drained

1 cup elbow macaroni

½ tsp. dried oregano

1 tsp. dried basil

¼ tsp. salt

½ tsp. freshly cracked black pepper

¼ cup grated Parmesan cheese

1. In a large stock pot over medium heat, heat extra-virgin olive oil.

2. Add white onion, garlic, and celery, and cook for 5 minutes or until lightly browned.

3. Add zucchini, green beans, carrot, and diced tomatoes, and cook for 1 or 2 more minutes.

4. Stir in vegetable broth, water, cannellini beans, elbow macaroni, oregano, basil, salt, and black pepper, and simmer for about 25 to 30 minutes or until vegetables and macaroni are tender.

5. Stir in Parmesan cheese, and serve hot.

Make ahead and freeze: Prepare up to end of step 4 up to 6 days ahead. Freeze in individual containers after step 4 for up to 2 months.

NUTRITION PER SERVING			
CALORIES	350	FAT	9g
CARBOHYDRATES	52g	CHOLESTEROL	5mg
SUGARS	13g	SODIUM	860mg
DIETARY FIBER	10g	VITAMIN C	60%
PROTEIN	14g	VITAMIN A	90%
		IRON	20%

Egg Drop **Soup**

This classic Asian soup will help rehydrate your body and give you a little extra boost of protein at the same time.

●　●　●　●　**Easy**

PREP 5 mins
COOK about 5 to 10 mins

YIELD 2 servings

INGREDIENTS

1 qt. (1l) low-sodium
　chicken broth
¼ tsp. salt
⅛ tsp. ground ginger
2 TB. fresh chives, chopped
1½ TB. cornstarch
2 large eggs
1 large egg white

1　In a large saucepan over high heat, heat 3¼ cups chicken broth. Stir in salt, ginger, and chives, and bring to a boil.

2　In a small bowl, stir together remaining chicken broth and cornstarch until smooth.

3　In another small bowl, whisk together eggs and egg white.

4　Using a fork, drizzle eggs a little at a time into boiling broth mixture.

5　Gradually stir in cornstarch mixture until soup is the desired consistency.

6　Serve hot.

Make ahead and freeze: Prepare up to end of step 5 up to 6 days ahead. Freeze in individual containers after step 5 for up to 2 months.

To make this recipe vegetarian, use a low-sodium vegetable stock in place of the chicken stock.

NUTRITION PER SERVING			
CALORIES	110	FAT	5g
CARBOHYDRATES	3g	CHOLESTEROL	215mg
SUGARS	0g	SODIUM	520mg
DIETARY FIBER	0g	VITAMIN C	2%
PROTEIN	12g	VITAMIN A	8%
		IRON	8%

Italian Wedding **Soup**

Enjoy this quick, easy, and authentic Italian wedding soup
for lunch on busy competition days.

1 In a medium bowl, combine 90% lean ground beef, egg,
unseasoned breadcrumbs, Parmesan cheese, basil, and
onion powder. Shape mixture into ¾-inch (2cm) balls.

2 In a large saucepan over medium-high heat, bring
chicken broth to a boil. Stir in escarole, orzo pasta,
carrots, and meatballs.

3 Return to a boil, reduce heat to medium, and simmer,
covered, for 10 minutes or until pasta is al dente. Stir
frequently to prevent sticking.

4 Serve hot.

Make ahead and freeze: Prepare up to end of step 3
up to 6 days ahead. Freeze in individual containers
after step 3 for up to 2 months.

 **Intermediate**

PREP 15 to 20 mins
COOK about 15 mins

YIELD 4 servings

INGREDIENTS

½ lb. (225g) 90% lean ground beef

1 large egg, lightly beaten

2 TB. dry unseasoned
breadcrumbs

1 TB. grated Parmesan cheese

½ tsp. dried basil

½ tsp. onion powder

5¾ cups low-sodium chicken
broth

2 cups thinly sliced escarole

1 cup uncooked orzo pasta

1 medium carrot, finely chopped
(⅓ cup)

NUTRITION PER SERVING			
CALORIES	260	FAT	8g
CARBOHYDRATES	26g	CHOLESTEROL	90mg
SUGARS	2g	SODIUM	220mg
DIETARY FIBER	2g	VITAMIN C	4%
PROTEIN	21g	VITAMIN A	50%
		IRON	20%

Quick Tortellini **Salad**

This is a great salad to bring to a precompetition potluck. Double or triple the portion size to make a delicious vegetarian meal.

● ○ ○ **Easy**

PREP about 5 to 10 mins + 2 to 4 hours marinate time
COOK 5 to 10 mins

YIELD 21 servings

INGREDIENTS

2 (9-oz.; 255g) pkg. refrigerated three-cheese tortellini

1½ cups cherry tomatoes, halved

⅓ cup fresh basil, chopped

1 small red onion, chopped (½ cup)

½ cup balsamic vinaigrette dressing

⅓ cup water

1 TB. brown sugar, packed

1 large clove garlic, minced

1 Cook three-cheese tortellini according to the package directions. Drain and rinse with cold water.

2 In a large bowl, combine tortellini, cherry tomatoes, basil, and red onion.

3 In a small bowl, combine balsamic vinaigrette dressing, water, brown sugar, and garlic. Stir marinade well until combined.

4 Pour marinade over pasta, and toss gently to coat.

5 Cover and refrigerate for at least 2 to 4 hours.

6 Serve chilled.

Make ahead: Refrigerate for 3 to 5 days.

To change up the flavor, choose tortellini with different fillings. Also, this salad is tasty served warm. Try serving it immediately after preparation or heating it in a microwave-safe container.

NUTRITION PER SERVING			
CALORIES	90	FAT	3g
CARBOHYDRATES	14g	CHOLESTEROL	10mg
SUGARS	2g	SODIUM	150mg
DIETARY FIBER	1g	VITAMIN C	2%
PROTEIN	4g	VITAMIN A	2%
		IRON	2%

Easy Italian **Pasta Salad**

This light and lovely pasta salad with fresh peppers and onions and zesty pepperoni is a super side for any meal.

 ● ● ● **Easy**

PREP 10 mins + 1 or 2 hours marinate time
COOK about 8 mins

YIELD 12 servings

INGREDIENTS

1 (12-oz.; 340g) pkg. tri-colored rotini pasta

¾ lb. (340g) pepperoni, diced

½ medium green bell pepper, ribs and seeds removed, and diced

½ medium red bell pepper, ribs and seeds removed, and diced

½ medium red onion, diced

1 cup Italian salad dressing

1 (6-oz.; 170g) can sliced black olives, drained

8 oz. (225g) small fresh mozzarella balls, drained

2 (.7-oz.; 20g) pkg. dry Italian salad dressing mix

½ cup freshly grated Parmesan cheese

1 Bring a large pot of water to a boil over medium-high heat, and cook tri-colored rotini pasta for about 8 minutes or until al dente. Drain and rinse pasta with cold water until cool.

2 In a large bowl, combine pasta, pepperoni, green bell pepper, red bell pepper, red onion, Italian salad dressing, black olives, mozzarella balls, dry Italian salad dressing mix, and Parmesan cheese.

3 Refrigerate for at least 1 or 2 hours before serving.

Make ahead: Refrigerate for 3 to 5 days.

NUTRITION PER SERVING			
CALORIES	390	FAT	26g
CARBOHYDRATES	29g	CHOLESTEROL	40mg
SUGARS	6g	SODIUM	1,390mg
DIETARY FIBER	2g	VITAMIN C	15%
PROTEIN	14g	VITAMIN A	6%
		IRON	15%

Easy Slow Cooker **Pot Roast**

Who has time for pot roast? You do, with this easy recipe made with mushroom soup and onion soup mix. Put it together in the morning, and it'll be ready for dinner.

1 In a 6-quart (5.5l) or larger slow cooker, combine cream of mushroom soup, dry onion soup mix, and beef broth.

2 Place pot roast in the slow cooker, and coat with soup mixture.

3 Cover and cook on high for 3 or 4 hours or on low for 8 or 9 hours.

4 Stir, and serve immediately.

Storage: Refrigerate leftovers for 3 to 5 days.

 ● ○ ○ **Easy**

PREP 5 mins
COOK 3 to 9 hours

YIELD 12 servings

INGREDIENTS

2 (10.75-oz.; 305g) cans condensed low-sodium cream of mushroom soup

1 (1-oz.; 25g) pkg. dry onion soup mix

1¼ cups low-sodium beef broth

5½ lb. (2.5kg) pot roast

To bulk up this recipe a bit and make it a one-pot slow cooker meal, add 1 pound (450g) baby carrots, about 2 pounds (1kg) fingerling potatoes, and about 1 large onion, sliced, when you add the pot roast. No need to add any extra liquids. To lower the fat content, opt for reduced-fat cream of mushroom soup and trim off any fat around the outside of the roast.

NUTRITION PER SERVING			
CALORIES	510	FAT	28g
CARBOHYDRATES	5g	CHOLESTEROL	160mg
SUGARS	1g	SODIUM	560mg
DIETARY FIBER	1g	VITAMIN C	0%
PROTEIN	56g	VITAMIN A	0%
		IRON	25%

Simple Chicken **Marsala**

This quick chicken dish features fresh mushrooms and sweet marsala wine, making it hearty and satisfying without weighing you down.

 ● ● ◐ **Intermediate**

PREP 5 to 10 mins
COOK about 16 mins

YIELD 4 servings

INGREDIENTS

¼ cup all-purpose flour

½ tsp. garlic salt

¼ tsp. freshly cracked black pepper

1 tsp. fresh oregano

4 (4-oz.; 110g) boneless, skinless chicken breasts

2 TB. extra-virgin olive oil

1 cup sliced fresh button mushrooms

½ cup marsala wine

1 In a medium bowl, combine all-purpose flour, garlic salt, black pepper, and oregano.

2 Dredge both sides of chicken breasts in flour mixture until lightly coated. Set aside.

3 In a large skillet over medium heat, heat extra-virgin olive oil. Add chicken to the skillet, and pan-sear for 2 or 3 minutes or until lightly browned on one side.

4 Turn over chicken, add mushrooms, and cook for 2 or 3 more minutes or until other side of chicken is lightly browned. Stir mushrooms occasionally to ensure they cook evenly.

5 Pour marsala wine over chicken, cover the skillet, reduce heat to low, and simmer for 10 minutes or until chicken is cooked through.

6 Serve hot immediately.

Storage: Refrigerate leftovers for 3 to 5 days.

To make this recipe gluten free, choose a gluten-free flour instead of all-purpose.

NUTRITION PER SERVING			
CALORIES	240	FAT	9g
CARBOHYDRATES	10g	CHOLESTEROL	55mg
SUGARS	3g	SODIUM	220mg
DIETARY FIBER	0g	VITAMIN C	2%
PROTEIN	19g	VITAMIN A	0%
		IRON	4%

Homemade Hamburger **Casserole**

An excellent source of protein, this family classic is easy to make from scratch. It also contains plenty of carbs to maintain your energy.

1 In a large skillet over medium-high heat, cook 90% lean ground beef, stirring occasionally, for 5 to 10 minutes or until beef is browned. Drain any fat through a colander, and return beef to skillet.

2 Add 2% milk, beef broth, elbow macaroni, cornstarch, chili powder, garlic powder, sugar, salt, paprika, and cayenne, and stir.

3 Bring to a boil, reduce heat to medium-low, cover, and simmer for 10 to 12 minutes or until pasta is al dente.

4 Add cheddar cheese, and stir until combined.

5 Garnish with parsley, and serve hot.

Make ahead and freeze: Freeze after step 4 for up to 2 months. Thaw in refrigerator for 1 or 2 days before baking at 350°F (180°C) for about 45 minutes or until cooked through.

Storage: Refrigerate leftovers for 3 to 5 days.

 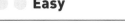 ● ○ ○ **Easy**

PREP 5 to 10 mins
COOK about 22 mins

YIELD 6 servings

INGREDIENTS

1 lb. (450g) 90% lean ground beef
2½ cups 2% milk
1 cup low-sodium beef broth
2 cups elbow macaroni
1 TB. cornstarch
1 TB. chili powder
2 tsp. garlic powder
1 tsp. sugar
1 tsp. salt
¾ tsp. paprika
¼ tsp. cayenne
2 cups shredded cheddar cheese
Fresh parsley, for garnish

To lower the fat, use the same amount of ground chicken or lean ground turkey instead of the ground beef.

Make this recipe gluten free easily by using a gluten-free elbow macaroni.

NUTRITION PER SERVING			
CALORIES	400	**FAT**	13g
CARBOHYDRATES	34g	**CHOLESTEROL**	65mg
SUGARS	6g	**SODIUM**	420mg
DIETARY FIBER	35g	**VITAMIN C**	2%
PROTEIN	35g	**VITAMIN A**	5%
		IRON	20%

Fantastic Fudge **Pops**

This is a great summertime snack to help you cool down after a long run and load up some carbs before your next big workout. In addition to the added carbs, these great homemade Fudge Pops have about 2 grams more protein than store bought.

● ● ● ● **Easy**

PREP 5 to 10 mins +
4 hours freeze time

YIELD 6 servings

INGREDIENTS

1 (3.9-oz.; 110g) pkg. chocolate
    instant pudding mix
2 cups cold whole milk
1 cup whipped topping, thawed

1 In a medium bowl, whisk together chocolate instant pudding mix and whole milk for about 1 or 2 minutes.

2 Gently fold in whipped topping.

3 Evenly divide pudding mix among 6 ice pop molds, and freeze for at least 4 hours or until firm.

Storage: Freeze leftovers for up to 1 week.

You can easily vary this recipe by using different flavors of instant pudding mix, like coconut cream or cookies and cream.

NUTRITION PER SERVING				
CALORIES	150	FAT	7g
CARBOHYDRATES	18g	CHOLESTEROL	10mg
SUGARS	18g	SODIUM	140mg
DIETARY FIBER	0g	VITAMIN C	0%
PROTEIN	3g	VITAMIN A	2%
		IRON	0%

Super-Satisfying Frozen Cherry Cheesecake **Pops**

This cool and creamy summertime snack stars with the taste of super-satisfying cheesecake.

● ○ ○ **Easy**

PREP 15 mins + 4 hours freeze time

YIELD 6 servings

INGREDIENTS

1 (3.9-oz.; 110g) pkg. cheesecake-flavored instant pudding mix

2 cups cold whole milk

1 cup whipped topping, thawed

½ cup cherry pie filling

1 In a medium bowl, whisk together cheesecake-flavored instant pudding mix and whole milk for about 1 or 2 minutes.

2 Gently fold in whipped topping.

3 Evenly divide cherry pie filling among 6 ice pop molds, and spoon pudding mix over top of cherry pie filling.

4 Freeze for at least 4 hours or until firm.

Storage: Freeze leftovers for up to 1 week.

You can easily change the flavor by using blueberry, strawberry, or even apple pie filling instead of cherry.

NUTRITION PER SERVING			
CALORIES	170	FAT	7g
CARBOHYDRATES	24g	CHOLESTEROL	10mg
SUGARS	18g	SODIUM	140mg
DIETARY FIBER	0g	VITAMIN C	2%
PROTEIN	3g	VITAMIN A	2%
		IRON	0%

Recipes for
Recovery

Now that your competition is over, it's time to let your body recover. To help with that, in Part 4, we share some tasty and easy-to-prepare recovery recipes, including high-carb recovery drinks and carry-along portables for eating immediately afterward, as well as soups, salads, entrées, side dishes, and desserts meant to help your body restock its nutrients and get you ready for your next big event.

And because the last thing you'll want to do after a big event is spend hours in the kitchen cooking, in this section, we offer good, homemade alternatives to store-bought foods that are quick and easy to prepare—some are as simple as dropping everything into a slow cooker and letting it cook.

We hope you relax and enjoy the bounty offered in this part's recovery recipes.

Pineapple Basil
Mojito

Rasberry Lemonade

Pineapple Basil **Mojito**

This sweet and delicious summery recovery cocktail is perfect for rehydrating your body after a long competition or workout.

  Easy

PREP 5 mins

YIELD 1 serving

INGREDIENTS

1 TB. sugar

⅛ tsp. salt

3 fresh basil leaves

½ cup pineapple juice

½ cup limeade

¾ cup club soda

1   In a large glass, combine sugar, salt, and basil leaves. Press ingredients together with the back of a spoon, or use a muddler, until basil leaves look a little bruised.

2   Add pineapple juice, limeade, and club soda, and stir to combine.

3   Drink immediately over ice.

NUTRITION PER SERVING			
CALORIES	170	FAT	0g
CARBOHYDRATES	42g	CHOLESTEROL	0mg
SUGARS	41g	SODIUM	300mg
DIETARY FIBER	0g	VITAMIN C	20%
PROTEIN	0g	VITAMIN A	0%
		IRON	2%

Raspberry **Lemonade**

Sweet raspberries and tart lemon juice combine in this refreshing beverage with a hint of honey. It's perfect for recovering after a hot race day.

 Easy

PREP 2 mins

YIELD 1 serving

INGREDIENTS

5 fresh raspberries

4 oz. (120ml) club soda

Juice of ½ lemon (about 1 TB.)

1 TB. honey

¼ cup coconut water

1   Place fresh raspberries in a bottle, and press with the back of a spoon, or use a muddler, until slightly mashed.

2   Add club soda, lemon juice, honey, and coconut water, and shake vigorously for about 30 seconds or until combined.

3   Serve over ice.

NUTRITION PER SERVING			
CALORIES	100	FAT	0g
CARBOHYDRATES	26g	CHOLESTEROL	0mg
SUGARS	18g	SODIUM	65mg
DIETARY FIBER	1g	VITAMIN C	35%
PROTEIN	1g	VITAMIN A	0%
		IRON	2%

Blueberry Lavender
Lemonade

This light and refreshing lemonade is full of good-for-you electrolytes.

 Intermediate

PREP 15 mins
COOK 5 mins

YIELD 1 serving

INGREDIENTS

⅛ cup water

⅛ cup sugar

⅛ cup dried lavender flowers

⅛ tsp. salt

¼ cup fresh blueberries

Juice of 2 medium lemons (¼ cup)

1 cup cold water

1   In 1-quart (1l) saucepan over medium heat, simmer sugar and water for about 5 minutes.

2   Place dried lavender flowers in a medium bowl, add sugar water, and set aside for 1 or 2 hours. Strain lavender water through a sieve.

3   In a large glass, press together salt and blueberries until blueberries are crushed slightly. Add lavender water, lemon juice, and cold water, and stir.

4   Serve over ice or chilled.

NUTRITION PER SERVING			
CALORIES	130	FAT	0g
CARBOHYDRATES	34g	CHOLESTEROL	0mg
SUGARS	28g	SODIUM	300mg
DIETARY FIBER	2g	VITAMIN C	60%
PROTEIN	0g	VITAMIN A	2%
		IRON	2%

Gingerade

This is a very light and refreshing beverage with soothing ginger, perfect to cool you off after a strenuous workout.

 Easy

PREP 5 mins

YIELD 1 serving

INGREDIENTS

1 (6-oz.; 175ml) can ginger ale
½ cup prepared lemonade
½ cup club soda
⅛ tsp. salt

1 In a water bottle, combine ginger ale, lemonade, club soda, and salt.

2 Drink over ice.

NUTRITION PER SERVING			
CALORIES	120	FAT	0g
CARBOHYDRATES	30g	CHOLESTEROL	0mg
SUGARS	29g	SODIUM	310mg
DIETARY FIBER	0g	VITAMIN C	0%
PROTEIN	0g	VITAMIN A	0%
		IRON	0%

Blueberry Banana
Recovery Smoothie

This is a simple, light, and creamy vegan smoothie that's perfect when you're not feeling like a heavy recovery beverage but still want something with a little substance.

 Easy

PREP 1 min

YIELD 2 servings

INGREDIENTS

1 small banana, peeled and sliced
1 cup fresh blueberries
1 cup almond milk
1 TB. sugar
½ cup ice cubes

1 In a blender, combine banana, blueberries, almond milk, sugar, and ice for about 1 minute or until completely combined.

2 Drink immediately.

NUTRITION PER SERVING			
CALORIES	100	FAT	1.5g
CARBOHYDRATES	23g	CHOLESTEROL	0mg
SUGARS	17g	SODIUM	50mg
DIETARY FIBER	2g	VITAMIN C	110%
PROTEIN	1g	VITAMIN A	4%
		IRON	2%

Kiwi Pineapple
Chia Smoothie

This is an excellent recovery smoothie. It's cool and refreshing with sweet kiwi and pineapple, plus the extra nutrition kick of chia seeds.

 Easy

PREP 5 mins

YIELD 3 servings

INGREDIENTS

2 cups fresh spinach
3 large kiwi, peeled and sliced (1 cup)
1 small banana, peeled and sliced
½ cup vanilla Greek yogurt
¼ cup fresh pineapple, chopped
¼ cup fresh orange juice
1 TB. chia seeds

1 In a blender, combine spinach, kiwi, banana, Greek yogurt, pineapple, orange juice, and chia seeds for about 1 minute or until completely combined.

2 Drink immediately.

NUTRITION PER SERVING			
CALORIES	160	FAT	5g
CARBOHYDRATES	25g	CHOLESTEROL	5mg
SUGARS	16g	SODIUM	40mg
DIETARY FIBER	4g	VITAMIN C	130%
PROTEIN	5g	VITAMIN A	15%
		IRON	6%

Kiwi Pineapple
Chia Smoothie

Blueberry Banana
Recovery Smoothie

Reduced-Fat **Tuna Melts**

Crave the classic tuna met but don't want all the fat? This much slimmer version is full of protein and carbs, not fat.

● ○ ○ **Easy**

PREP 10 mins
COOK 3 to 5 mins

YIELD 4 servings

INGREDIENTS

2 (5-oz.; 140g) cans chunk light tuna in water, drained

½ small red onion, diced

2 TB. reduced-fat mayonnaise

Juice of ½ medium lemon (about 1 TB.)

1 TB. fresh parsley, chopped

⅛ tsp. salt

1 tsp. spicy mustard

⅛ tsp. freshly cracked black pepper

4 slices whole-wheat bread, toasted

2 large roma tomatoes, sliced

4 slices sharp cheddar cheese

1 Preheat the broiler.

2 In a medium bowl, combine tuna, red onion, mayonnaise, lemon juice, parsley, salt, spicy mustard, and black pepper.

3 Spread about ¼ cup tuna mixture on each slice of toasted whole-wheat bread, and top with slices of roma tomatoes and sharp cheddar cheese.

4 Place sandwiches on a baking sheet, and broil for about 3 to 5 minutes or until cheese is bubbling and starting to turn golden brown.

5 Serve immediately.

Make ahead: Refrigerate after step 2 for up to 3 days for quicker assembly.

To make this recipe gluten free, select gluten-free bread.

NUTRITION PER SERVING			
CALORIES	300	FAT	13g
CARBOHYDRATES	26g	CHOLESTEROL	65mg
SUGARS	5g	SODIUM	65mg
DIETARY FIBER	8g	VITAMIN C	15%
PROTEIN	27g	VITAMIN A	15%
		IRON	6%

Mediterranean Salmon **Wraps**

Grilled salmon and a couscous salad made with delicious fresh herbs, vegetables, and citrus are all wrapped up in a tortilla for a delicious, on-the-go meal.

● ○ ○ **Easy**

PREP 10 mins
COOK 16 to 20 mins

YIELD 4 servings

INGREDIENTS

4 (4-oz.; 110g) skinless
  salmon fillets

⅓ cup water

⅓ cup couscous

¼ cup sun-dried tomatoes

1 cup fresh parsley, chopped

½ cup fresh mint, chopped

Juice of 2 medium lemons
  (¼ cup)

3 TB. extra-virgin olive oil

2 tsp. minced garlic

¼ tsp. salt

¼ tsp. freshly cracked
  black pepper

4 (10-in.; 25cm) flour tortillas

4 leaves red leaf lettuce

1 medium cucumber, sliced
  (1 cup)

1 Set a medium sauté pan over medium heat, and lightly spray grill with cooking spray.

2 Place salmon fillets in the pan, and cook for 6 to 8 minutes on each side or until fish flakes easily with a fork. Remove from the grill, and set aside.

3 Meanwhile, in a small saucepan over medium-high heat, bring water to a boil. Add couscous, stir, and remove the pan from heat.

4 Add sun-dried tomatoes, cover, and allow to sit for 5 minutes. Fluff with a fork, and set aside.

5 In a small bowl, combine parsley, mint, lemon juice, extra-virgin olive oil, garlic, salt, and black pepper. Add to couscous, stir, and set aside.

6 Evenly divide couscous mixture among tortillas, spread into a thin layer, and top with red leaf lettuce. Divide salmon among wraps, and top with cucumber slices. Roll each wrap like a burrito, cut in half, and enjoy warm or chilled.

Make ahead: Prepare up to 3 days ahead, and refrigerate.

NUTRITION PER SERVING			
CALORIES	650	FAT	31g
CARBOHYDRATES	60g	CHOLESTEROL	60mg
SUGARS	2g	SODIUM	640mg
DIETARY FIBER	4g	VITAMIN C	60%
PROTEIN	33g	VITAMIN A	30%
		IRON	25%

Mini Apple **Pies**

These tasty little pies are portion controlled. They're quick and easy to make ahead for lunches or grab-and-go snacks.

1 Preheat the oven to 425°F (220°C).

2 Unroll piecrust onto your work surface. Using a large round cookie cutter (2½ or 3 inches; 6.25 to 7.5cm), cut out rounds. Gather scraps, reroll with a rolling pin, and cut out more rounds until you have a total of 10. Press each crust round into the cup of an ungreased muffin pan.

3 In a medium bowl, combine Honeycrisp apples, sugar, brown sugar, all-purpose flour, cinnamon, salt, and vanilla extract. Divide mixture evenly among crust-lined muffin cups.

4 Bake for 18 to 20 minutes or until crusts are golden brown and apple mixture is bubbly. Allow to cool completely in the pan for about 30 minutes.

5 With a knife, loosen edges of crusts, and remove pies from the pan.

6 Allow pies to cool for about 25 to 30 minutes before serving. Store leftovers in an airtight container in a cool space or in the refrigerator.

Make ahead and freeze: Prepare up to end of step 3 up to 3 days ahead. Freeze after step 3 for up to 2 months. Thaw in refrigerator for 1 day before baking.

 ● ○ ○ **Easy**

PREP 10 mins
COOK 18 to 20 mins + 30 mins cool time

YIELD 10 servings

INGREDIENTS

1 (9-in.; 23cm) premade piecrust, softened

2 large Honeycrisp apples, peeled, cored, and finely diced

1 TB. sugar

1 TB. light brown sugar, packed

1 TB. all-purpose flour

½ tsp. ground cinnamon

⅛ tsp. salt

1 tsp. vanilla extract

NUTRITION PER SERVING			
CALORIES	110	FAT	4.5g
CARBOHYDRATES	17g	CHOLESTEROL	0mg
SUGARS	8g	SODIUM	100mg
DIETARY FIBER	1g	VITAMIN C	2%
PROTEIN	1g	VITAMIN A	0%
		IRON	2%

Mini Sweet Potato **Pies**

These pies make a great mini dessert or snack with rich spice flavors that will warm you up after a brisk autumn workout.

● ○ ○ **Easy**

PREP 10 mins
COOK 40 mins

YIELD 10 servings

INGREDIENTS

1 (9-in.; 23cm) premade piecrust, softened

2 large eggs

½ cup light brown sugar, packed

1 tsp. ground cinnamon

½ tsp. ground cloves

½ tsp. ground ginger

½ tsp. vanilla extract

⅛ tsp. salt

½ cup 2% milk

15 oz. (420g) mashed sweet potato (about 2 medium sweet potatoes)

1 Preheat the oven to 350°F (180°C).

2 Unroll piecrust onto your work surface. Using a large round cookie cutter (2½ or 3 inches; 6.25 to 7.5cm), cut out rounds. Gather scraps, reroll with a rolling pin, and cut out more rounds until you have a total of 10. Press each crust round into the cup of an ungreased muffin pan.

3 In a large bowl, and using a rubber spatula, beat together eggs, brown sugar, cinnamon, cloves, ginger, vanilla extract, salt, 2% milk, and sweet potato until smooth. Evenly divide dough among muffin cups, filling each cup to top of dough.

4 Bake for 25 to 30 minutes or until a toothpick inserted in the center comes out clean. Allow to cool in the pan for about 10 minutes.

5 With a knife, loosen edges of crusts, and remove pies from the pan.

6 Allow pies to cool for about 25 to 30 minutes before serving. Store leftovers in an airtight container in a cool space or in the refrigerator.

Make ahead and freeze: Prepare up to end of step 3 up to 3 days ahead. Freeze after step 3 for up to 2 months. Thaw in refrigerator for 1 day before baking.

NUTRITION PER SERVING			
CALORIES	170	FAT	6g
CARBOHYDRATES	27g	CHOLESTEROL	45mg
SUGARS	14g	SODIUM	135mg
DIETARY FIBER	2g	VITAMIN C	10%
PROTEIN	3g	VITAMIN A	130%
		IRON	4%

Easy Slow Cooker Pumpkin Pie
Rice Pudding

This warm and filling treat is easy to prepare in the colder months to get in a few extra carbs for those winter sports.

● ○ ○ **Easy**

PREP 5 mins
COOK about 5 hours

YIELD 10 servings

INGREDIENTS

2 cups short-grain white rice (not quick cooking)

1 (12-oz; 340g) can fat-free evaporated milk

2 cups canned pumpkin

3¼ cups 2% milk

½ cup light brown sugar, packed

1 TB. pumpkin pie spice

¼ tsp. salt

1 tsp. vanilla extract

⅓ cup raisins

1 Lightly coat the inside of a 3-quart (3l) slow cooker with cooking spray.

2 In the slow cooker, combine white rice, evaporated milk, pumpkin, 2% milk, brown sugar, pumpkin pie spice, salt, vanilla extract, and raisins.

3 Cover, and cook on low for about 5 hours or until rice is tender.

4 Serve warm.

Storage: Refrigerate leftovers for 3 to 5 days.

NUTRITION PER SERVING			
CALORIES	290	FAT	2g
CARBOHYDRATES	60g	CHOLESTEROL	5mg
SUGARS	26g	SODIUM	135mg
DIETARY FIBER	4g	VITAMIN C	0%
PROTEIN	8g	VITAMIN A	140%
		IRON	15%

Chocolate Peanut Butter **Bars**

These bars are super tasty and perfect for a hearty snack after a big game.

● ○ ○ **Easy**

PREP 3 hours, 15 mins
COOK 1 to 3 mins

YIELD 8 servings

INGREDIENTS

½ cup unsalted butter, melted

1 cup graham cracker crumbs

1 cup confectioners' sugar

¾ cup plus 2 TB. creamy
      peanut butter

1 cup 60% dark chocolate chips

To make this recipe gluten free, use gluten-free graham crackers.

1 Line an 8×8-inch (20×20cm) square baking pan with aluminum foil.

2 In a medium bowl, combine unsalted butter, graham cracker crumbs, and confectioners' sugar.

3 Stir in ¾ cup peanut butter, and spread mixture into the bottom of the prepared baking pan.

4 In a small, microwave-safe bowl, microwave remaining 2 tablespoons peanut butter with 60% dark chocolate chips for 1 to 3 minutes or until melted. Stir until smooth, and spread over peanut butter layer.

5 Chill for at least 3 hours or until completely firm.

6 Allow to sit at room temperature for 10 minutes before cutting into 16 bars.

7 Serve chilled.

Make ahead: Prepare up to step 7, and refrigerate in an airtight container for up to 1 week.

NUTRITION PER SERVING			
CALORIES	260	FAT	18g
CARBOHYDRATES	23g	CHOLESTEROL	15mg
SUGARS	14g	SODIUM	115mg
DIETARY FIBER	2g	VITAMIN C	0%
PROTEIN	5g	VITAMIN A	4%
		IRON	2%

Cherries Jubilee **Bars**

These cherry bars are an easy, summery treat that give you something sweet without breaking your daily calorie budget.

1 Preheat the oven to 325°F (170°C).

2 In a large bowl, and using an electric mixer on low speed, beat cherry cake mix, unsalted butter, and vegetable oil for 1 or 2 minutes or until crumbly. Reserve 1 cup crumb mixture.

3 Press remaining crumb mixture in the bottom of an ungreased 9×13-inch (23×33cm) baking pan.

4 In the same large bowl, and using an electric mixer on medium speed, beat cream cheese and cherry frosting for 1 to 3 minutes or until smooth. Beat in eggs and egg whites until blended.

5 Pour filling over crust, and sprinkle with reserved crumb mixture.

6 Bake for about 45 minutes or until set. Allow to cool completely.

7 Cover and refrigerate at least 2 hours until chilled before cutting into 6 rows by 6. Store leftovers covered in the refrigerator.

Make ahead: Prepare up to step 6, and refrigerate in an airtight container for up to 1 week.

 ● ● ●   **Easy**

PREP 20 mins
COOK 3 hours, 5 mins

YIELD 36 servings

INGREDIENTS

1 box cherry cake mix
¼ cup unsalted butter
¼ cup vegetable oil
2 (8-oz.; 225g) pkg. reduced-fat cream cheese, softened
16 oz. (450g) cherry frosting
2 large eggs
2 large egg whites

NUTRITION PER SERVING			
CALORIES	116	FAT	8g
CARBOHYDRATES	11g	CHOLESTEROL	20mg
SUGARS	9g	SODIUM	100mg
DIETARY FIBER	0g	VITAMIN C	0%
PROTEIN	2g	VITAMIN A	2%
		IRON	0%

If you can't find cherry cake mix or cherry frosting, use whichever combination of flavors you prefer.

Vegetable **Stew**

This is the quickest and easiest vegetable stew you will ever make. It's ideal for a cold winter day and when you need to get in a few extra carbs.

● ○ ○ **Easy**

PREP 10 mins
COOK about 30 mins

YIELD 4 servings

INGREDIENTS

1 TB. extra-virgin olive oil

1 medium sweet onion, diced

2 medium carrots, peeled and diced

2 medium parsnips, peeled and diced

2 medium celery stalks, diced

3 cups vegetable broth

2 cups canned, diced tomatoes, drained

3 oz. (85g) tomato paste

2 cups canned butter beans, drained and rinsed

½ cup fresh parsley, chopped

1 In a medium soup pot over medium heat, heat extra-virgin olive oil. Add sweet onion, and cook for about 5 minutes or until translucent.

2 Add carrots, parsnips, and celery to the pot, cover, and cook for about 5 minutes.

3 Add vegetable broth, tomatoes, and tomato paste to the pot, and bring to a boil.

4 Cover, reduce heat to medium-low, and simmer for about 10 minutes.

5 Stir in butter beans, and cook for 5 more minutes or until vegetables are tender.

6 Stir in parsley, and serve hot.

Make ahead and freeze: Prepare up to end of step 5 up to 6 days ahead. Freeze in individual containers after step 5 for up to 2 months.

To lower the sodium in your stew, use a reduced-sodium or low-sodium vegetable broth.

NUTRITION PER SERVING			
CALORIES	240	FAT	4g
CARBOHYDRATES	48g	CHOLESTEROL	0mg
SUGARS	17g	SODIUM	1,280mg
DIETARY FIBER	12g	VITAMIN C	70%
PROTEIN	10g	VITAMIN A	160%
		IRON	25%

Hearty Legume **Soup**

This filling soup is bursting with flavor. It's excellent to warm up with after a cold game day.

● ○ ○ **Easy**

PREP 10 to 15 mins
COOK about 45 mins

YIELD 2 servings

INGREDIENTS

2 cups low-sodium chicken broth

1 (12-oz.; 350ml) can amber beer

½ cup dried lentils, sorted and rinsed

1 medium carrot, diced

1 medium celery stalk, diced

1 small white onion, chopped

1 (5-in.; 12.5cm) fully cooked smoked Polish sausage, sliced

1 TB. fresh basil leaves

¼ tsp. freshly cracked black pepper

1 bay leaf

2 TB. freshly grated Parmesan cheese

1 In a large pot over medium-high heat, bring chicken broth, amber beer, and lentils to a boil. Reduce heat to medium-low, cover, and simmer, stirring occasionally, for about 20 to 25 minutes or until lentils are tender.

2 Stir in carrot, celery, white onion, smoked Polish sausage, basil, black pepper, and bay leaf. Cover, and simmer, stirring occasionally, for 20 minutes. Remove bay leaf.

3 Serve hot with Parmesan cheese sprinkled on top.

Make ahead and freeze: Prepare up to end of step 2 up to 6 days ahead. Freeze in individual containers after step 2 for up to 2 months.

NUTRITION PER SERVING			
CALORIES	480	FAT	19g
CARBOHYDRATES	42g	CHOLESTEROL	45mg
SUGARS	4g	SODIUM	690mg
DIETARY FIBER	9g	VITAMIN C	10%
PROTEIN	23g	VITAMIN A	130%
		IRON	25%

Turkey **Chili**

This is a wonderful spicy turkey chili, with tons of protein and lots of flavor.

1 In a large pot over medium heat, heat extra-virgin olive oil. Add red bell pepper, yellow onion, and garlic, and cook, stirring occasionally, for about 5 to 8 minutes or until vegetables have softened.

2 Increase heat to medium-high, add turkey, and cook, breaking up meat into smaller pieces with a spoon, for about 4 to 6 minutes or until turkey is no longer pink and is cooked through.

3 Add chili powder, salt, oregano, cumin, cayenne, and cinnamon, and cook, stirring occasionally, for about 1 minute.

4 Add tomatoes with juice and vegetable broth, and bring to a simmer.

5 Add cannellini beans, return to a simmer, reduce heat to medium-low, and add bay leaf. Simmer, stirring occasionally, for about 30 minutes.

6 Remove bay leaf, and serve hot.

Make ahead and freeze: Prepare up to end of step 5 up to 6 days ahead. Freeze in individual containers after step 5 for up to 2 months.

  Easy

PREP 10 mins
COOK 45 mins

YIELD 6 servings

INGREDIENTS

2 TB. extra-virgin olive oil

1 medium red bell pepper, ribs and seeds removed, and diced

1 medium yellow onion, ribs and seeds removed, and diced

2 medium cloves garlic, minced

1 lb. (450g) lean ground turkey

3 TB. chili powder

2 tsp. salt

½ tsp. dried oregano

½ tsp. ground cumin

⅛ tsp. cayenne

⅛ tsp. ground cinnamon

1 (28-oz.; 800g) can diced tomatoes, with juice

1 cup low-sodium vegetable broth

2 (14-oz.; 400g) cans cannellini beans, drained and rinsed

1 bay leaf

To lower the sodium, omit the salt, use dried beans (the preparation will change), or pick low-sodium tomatoes and beans, drained and rinsed.

NUTRITION PER SERVING			
CALORIES	310	FAT	10g
CARBOHYDRATES	32g	CHOLESTEROL	45mg
SUGARS	8g	SODIUM	1,530mg
DIETARY FIBER	9g	VITAMIN C	70%
PROTEIN	25g	VITAMIN A	40%
		IRON	25%

Seafood **Chowder**

This chowder, which is similar to a New England clam chowder, is a warm and hearty meal you can enjoy with your family or the whole team—and it won't skyrocket your calorie intake.

1 In a large stockpot over medium heat, cook bacon for 2 to 5 minutes or until browned.

2 Add yellow onions, and cook for 10 minutes.

3 Add all-purpose flour, and stir until well combined.

4 Add clam juice, white potatoes, thyme, salt, and black pepper; bring to a simmer; and cook for about 10 minute or until potatoes are almost fork-tender.

5 Add clams, haddock, shrimp, sea scallops, and oysters, and simmer for 10 minutes.

6 Add 2% milk, and heat through.

7 Serve hot immediately.

Make ahead and freeze: Prepare up to end of step 6 up to 6 days ahead. Freeze in individual containers after step 6 for up to 2 months.

● ○ ○ **Easy**

PREP 20 mins
COOK 45 mins

YIELD 12 servings

INGREDIENTS

1 (6-oz.; 170g) slab bacon, cut into ½-in. (1.25cm) pieces

2 large yellow onions, diced

¼ cup all-purpose flour

2 cups clam juice

4 medium white potatoes, peeled and diced

1½ tsp. fresh thyme

1 tsp. salt

½ tsp. freshly cracked black pepper

½ lb. (225g) shucked clams

½ lb. (225g) haddock, cut into ¾-in. (2cm) chunks

½ lb. (225g) shrimp (18 to 20 count), peeled and deveined

½ lb. (225g) sea scallops

½ lb. (225g) shucked oysters

1 qt. (1l) 2% milk

To make this recipe gluten free, opt for a gluten-free flour.

NUTRITION PER SERVING			
CALORIES	250	FAT	9g
CARBOHYDRATES	22g	CHOLESTEROL	80mg
SUGARS	6g	SODIUM	570mg
DIETARY FIBER	2g	VITAMIN C	20%
PROTEIN	20g	VITAMIN A	4%
		IRON	30%

Mediterranean **Quinoa Salad**

This protein-packed salad with fresh citrus and vegetables is just right for a quick bite after the gym—and it's a hit at parties! To save time, chop the vegetables while the quinoa is cooking.

● ○ ○ **Easy**

PREP 10 mins
COOK 15 mins + 1 or 2
      hours cool time

YIELD 6 servings

INGREDIENTS

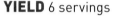

2 cups water

1 cup quinoa

1 small red onion, diced (¼ cup)

Juice of 1 medium lemon

¼ cup kalamata olives, pitted
  and sliced

2 TB. extra-virgin olive oil

2 medium cucumbers, peeled,
  seeded, and diced (2 cups)

1 cup cherry tomatoes, halved

⅓ cup crumbled feta cheese

¼ cup fresh parsley, chopped

1 tsp. salt

½ tsp. freshly cracked
  black pepper

1 Rinse quinoa thoroughly for about 30 seconds.

2 In a medium pot over medium-high heat, bring water and quinoa to a boil. Reduce heat to low, cover, and simmer for 15 minutes.

3 Remove from heat, and keep quinoa covered for 5 minutes.

4 Fluff quinoa with a fork, and pour into a large bowl to cool for 10 to 15 minutes.

5 Add red onion, lemon juice, kalamata olives, extra-virgin olive oil, cucumber, cherry tomatoes, feta cheese, parsley, salt, and black pepper, and stir to combine.

6 Refrigerate for 1 or 2 hours before serving.

Make ahead: Prepare up to 3 to 5 days ahead, and refrigerate.

For an Italian twist, swap about 1 cup diced fresh mozzarella for the feta cheese, add chopped fresh basil, and ½ cup of your favorite Italian dressing.

NUTRITION PER SERVING			
CALORIES	200	FAT	9g
CARBOHYDRATES	24g	CHOLESTEROL	0mg
SUGARS	4g	SODIUM	650mg
DIETARY FIBER	4g	VITAMIN C	20%
PROTEIN	7g	VITAMIN A	15%
		IRON	10%

Super-Simple **Couscous Salad**

This delicious salad, tossed with creamy pesto and tangy feta cheese, is perfect for providing the carbs you need, with a powerful punch of protein.

1 Place couscous in a large bowl.

2 In a microwave-safe measuring cup, microwave water for 5 to 8 minutes or until boiling. Pour over couscous, set aside for 10 minutes or until water has been absorbed and couscous is fluffy.

3 After couscous has "cooked," allow to cool to room temperature.

4 Add scallions, red bell pepper, cucumber, feta cheese, pesto sauce, pine nuts, salt, and black pepper, and stir with a fork to combine.

5 Allow to chill in the refrigerator for 1 or 2 hours before serving.

Make ahead: Prepare up to 3 to 5 days ahead, and refrigerate.

If you don't have time to chop your own vegetables, shop your grocery's produce section for prechopped vegetables—or try the salad bar.

  Easy

PREP 5 to 10 mins
COOK about 18 mins + 1 or 2 hours cool time

YIELD 4 SERVINGS

INGREDIENTS

3.5 oz. (100g) couscous

1 cup water

2 scallions, sliced

1 small red bell pepper, ribs and seeds removed, and diced

½ medium cucumber, seeded and diced

2 oz. (55g) crumbled feta cheese

2 TB. pesto sauce

2 TB. pine nuts

½ tsp. salt

¼ tsp freshly cracked black pepper

Use quinoa instead of couscous for a gluten-free dish. To prepare, bring 2 cups water to a boil in a medium saucepan over medium-high heat. Add 1 cup quinoa, cover, reduce heat to low, and simmer for 5 to 10 minutes.

NUTRITION PER SERVING			
CALORIES	200	FAT	8g
CARBOHYDRATES	24g	CHOLESTEROL	5mg
SUGARS	2g	SODIUM	560mg
DIETARY FIBER	3g	VITAMIN C	50%
PROTEIN	9g	VITAMIN A	20%
		IRON	6%

Marinated Greek **Orzo Salad**

This refreshing salad combines the flavors of zesty lemon and classic Italian herbs with crunchy fresh vegetables.

● ○ ○ **Easy**

PREP 5 to 10 mins
COOK 10 mins
+ 1 hour chill time

YIELD 6 servings

INGREDIENTS

1½ cups orzo pasta

2 (6-oz.; 170g) cans marinated artichoke hearts, drained with liquid reserved

1 medium tomato, seeded and diced

1 medium cucumber, seeded and diced

1 small red onion, diced

1 cup crumbled feta cheese

1 (2-oz.; 55g) can sliced black olives, drained

¼ cup fresh parsley, chopped

Juice of ½ medium lemon (1 TB.)

½ tsp. fresh oregano

½ tsp. lemon pepper seasoning

1 Fill a large pot with water, set over medium-high heat, and bring to a boil. Add orzo pasta, and cook for 8 to 10 minutes or until al dente.

2 In a large bowl, combine orzo pasta, artichoke hearts, tomato, cucumber, red onion, feta cheese, black olives, parsley, lemon juice, oregano, and lemon pepper seasoning. Refrigerate for at least 1 hour.

3 Before serving, drizzle reserved artichoke marinade over salad, and toss to coat.

Make ahead: Prepare up to 3 to 5 days ahead, and refrigerate.

For an Italian twist on this recipe, omit the cucumber, parsley, and feta, and substitute 1 cup diced mozzarella cheese, ¼ cup chopped fresh cilantro, and 2 seeded and diced avocados.

NUTRITION PER SERVING			
CALORIES	250	FAT	10g
CARBOHYDRATES	10g	CHOLESTEROL	20mg
SUGARS	5g	SODIUM	600mg
DIETARY FIBER	4g	VITAMIN C	40%
PROTEIN	10g	VITAMIN A	10%
		IRON	10%

Chickpea, Tomato, and Mozzarella
Salad with Pesto

This delicious take on the classic tomato and mozzarella salad is packed with protein, fiber, carbs, and electrolytes for recovery.

  ● ○ ○ **Easy**

PREP 5 to 10 mins

YIELD 4 servings

INGREDIENTS

1 (15-oz.; 420g) can chickpeas, drained and rinsed

¼ cup pesto sauce

1 cup cherry tomatoes, halved

½ cup small fresh mozzarella balls, cut in half

½ tsp. salt

¼ tsp. freshly cracked black pepper

2 TB. fresh basil, chopped

1 In a medium bowl, gently combine chickpeas, pesto sauce, cherry tomatoes, mozzarella cheese, salt, and black pepper.

2 Garnish with fresh basil, and serve chilled.

Make ahead: Prepare up to 3 to 5 days ahead, and refrigerate.

NUTRITION PER SERVING			
CALORIES	290	FAT	18g
CARBOHYDRATES	17g	CHOLESTEROL	40mg
SUGARS	3g	SODIUM	550mg
DIETARY FIBER	5g	VITAMIN C	10%
PROTEIN	15g	VITAMIN A	10%
		IRON	10%

White Beans and **Broccoli**

With fresh garlic and zesty pepper flakes, this dish is full of protein and packed with carbs, thanks to the beans and broccoli.

1 Trim and discard leaves and tough stem from broccoli, cut off florets, peel large stems, and cut into 1½-inch (3.75cm) pieces. Rinse and drain.

2 In a large skillet over medium heat, heat extra-virgin olive oil. Add garlic, and cook for 1 or 2 minutes or until lightly golden.

3 Add broccoli, chicken broth, crushed red pepper flakes, salt, and black pepper, and cook, stirring occasionally, for about 3 minutes.

4 Add cannellini beans, and cook, stirring occasionally, for about 5 minutes or until broccoli is just tender and beans are cooked through.

5 Meanwhile, bring a large pot of water to boil over medium-high heat. Add orecchiette pasta, and cook for about 8 minutes or until al dente. Drain pasta, add to broccoli mixture, and toss to combine.

6 Serve hot.

Storage: Refrigerate leftovers for 3 to 5 days.

● ● ○ **Intermediate**

PREP 10 mins
COOK 15 mins

YIELD 6 servings

INGREDIENTS

1½ lb. (680g) broccoli

2 TB. extra-virgin olive oil

2 cloves garlic, minced

⅓ cup low-sodium chicken broth

¼ tsp. crushed red pepper flakes

½ tsp. salt

¼ tsp. freshly cracked black pepper

2 (14-oz.; 400g) cans cannellini beans, drained and rinsed

1 lb. (450g) orecchiette pasta

NUTRITION PER SERVING			
CALORIES	460	FAT	6g
CARBOHYDRATES	82g	CHOLESTEROL	0mg
SUGARS	7g	SODIUM	580mg
DIETARY FIBER	9g	VITAMIN C	170%
PROTEIN	23g	VITAMIN A	150%
		IRON	30%

To make this dish vegetarian, use low-sodium vegetable broth instead of chicken broth.

Basil Penne Pasta with
Asparagus and Feta

Fresh basil, asparagus, and cherry tomatoes will have you thinking of summer with each bite of this tasty dish.

 Easy

PREP 10 mins
COOK 16 mins

YIELD 4 servings

INGREDIENTS

2 cups penne pasta

1 lb. (450g) fresh asparagus, trimmed and cut into 1½-in. (3.75cm) pieces

2 TB. extra-virgin olive oil

2 cloves garlic, finely chopped

1 (15-oz.; 420g) can cannellini beans, drained and rinsed

1½ cups cherry tomatoes, halved

¼ cup fresh basil leaves, chopped

2 TB. fresh lemon juice

½ tsp. salt

¼ tsp. freshly cracked black pepper

1 (6-oz.; 170g) pkg. crumbled feta cheese

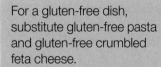

For a gluten-free dish, substitute gluten-free pasta and gluten-free crumbled feta cheese.

1 Fill a large pot with water, set over medium-high heat, and bring to a boil. Add penne pasta, and cook for about 8 minutes or until al dente. During the last 3 minutes of cook time, add asparagus.

2 Meanwhile, in a large skillet over medium heat, heat extra-virgin olive oil. Add garlic, and cook, stirring occasionally, for about 3 minutes.

3 Add cannellini beans, cherry tomatoes, basil, lemon juice, salt, and black pepper, and toss gently.

4 Stir cooked pasta and asparagus into the skillet, and cook, stirring occasionally, for about 5 minutes or until heated through.

5 Stir in feta cheese, and serve hot.

Storage: Refrigerate leftovers for 3 to 5 days.

NUTRITION PER SERVING			
CALORIES	460	FAT	17g
CARBOHYDRATES	56g	CHOLESTEROL	40mg
SUGARS	9g	SODIUM	1,050mg
DIETARY FIBER	9g	VITAMIN C	30%
PROTEIN	21g	VITAMIN A	30%
		IRON	30%

Lean Steak and Brown Rice
Stir-Fry

This is a simple stir-fry dish you can make in a hurry. Feed the whole family, or save the leftovers for meals later in the week.

1 In a medium saucepan over high heat, bring water and brown rice to a boil. Reduce heat to medium-low, cover, and simmer for 50 minutes. Remove from heat, and set aside.

2 Meanwhile, trim fat from sirloin steak, and cut steak into thin strips.

3 In a large skillet over medium-high heat, heat extra-virgin olive oil. Add garlic, and sauté for 1 or 2 minutes or until golden brown.

4 Add steak, red wine vinegar, salt, black pepper, crushed red pepper flakes, and fresh thyme, and cook, stirring occasionally, for about 6 minutes or until beef is browned.

5 Add onion and tomato, and cook for 3 to 5 minutes or until onions are transparent.

6 Stir in rice until well combined, and serve immediately.

Storage: Refrigerate leftovers for 3 to 5 days.

● ○ ○ **Easy**

PREP 10 mins
COOK about 1 hour

YIELD 6 servings

INGREDIENTS

4 cups water

2 cups brown rice

1 lb. (450g) sirloin steak

2 TB. extra-virgin olive oil

1 clove garlic, minced

½ tsp. red wine vinegar

½ tsp. salt

¼ tsp. freshly cracked
    black pepper

¼ tsp. crushed red pepper flakes

¼ tsp. fresh thyme

1 small sweet onion, sliced

1 medium tomato, diced

NUTRITION PER SERVING			
CALORIES	440	FAT	14g
CARBOHYDRATES	50g	CHOLESTEROL	55mg
SUGARS	2g	SODIUM	150mg
DIETARY FIBER	3g	VITAMIN C	8%
PROTEIN	27g	VITAMIN A	6%
		IRON	15%

To make this recipe vegetarian, use 1 lb. (450g) extra-firm tofu, cut into ½×½-inch (1.25×1.25cm) cubes. Add tofu at the same time the steak would be added, and continue recipe as directed.

Zucchini Pizza **Casserole**

This family-size recipe bakes vegetables in a filling casserole with the classic cheesiness of pizza. It's quick, easy to prepare, and delicious!

● ○ ○ **Easy**

PREP 2 mins
COOK 1 hour, 5 mins

YIELD 8 servings

INGREDIENTS

6 medium zucchini, shredded (4 cups)

½ tsp. salt

2 large eggs

½ tsp. freshly cracked black pepper

½ tsp. crushed red pepper flakes

½ cup grated Parmesan cheese

2 cups shredded part-skim mozzarella cheese

1 cup shredded cheddar cheese

1 lb. (450g) 90% lean ground beef

1 small yellow onion, diced

1 (15-oz.; 420g) can tomato sauce

1 medium green bell pepper, ribs and seeds removed, and diced

To make this recipe vegetarian, omit the ground beef. (Feel free to substitute any meat alternatives, such as tofu or seitan, to bring up the protein value.)

1 Preheat the oven to 400°F (200°C). Lightly grease a 9×13-inch (23×33cm) baking pan with cooking spray.

2 Place shredded zucchini in a strainer, sprinkle with salt, and set aside for 10 minutes. Squeeze out excess moisture.

3 In the prepared baking pan, combine zucchini, eggs, black pepper, crushed red pepper flakes, Parmesan cheese, and half of mozzarella cheese and cheddar cheese. Press mixture into the bottom of the pan.

4 Bake, uncovered, for 20 minutes.

5 Meanwhile, in a medium sauté pan over medium heat, cook ground beef and yellow onion for 5 to 10 minutes or until meat is no longer pink. Drain off any fat.

6 Add tomato sauce, stir to combine, and spoon sauce over zucchini mixture. Sprinkle with remaining mozzarella cheese and cheddar cheese, and add green bell pepper. Bake for 20 minutes or until heated through.

7 Allow to rest for about 8 to 10 minutes before serving.

Make ahead and freeze: Prepare up to end of step 3 up to 6 days ahead. Freeze after step 6 for up to 2 months. Thaw in refrigerator for 1 or 2 days before baking.

NUTRITION PER SERVING			
CALORIES	250	FAT	10g
CARBOHYDRATES	10g	CHOLESTEROL	105mg
SUGARS	4g	SODIUM	910mg
DIETARY FIBER	3g	VITAMIN C	90%
PROTEIN	31g	VITAMIN A	25%
		IRON	15%

Garlic Chicken with Orzo **Pasta**

This delicious and simple chicken dish—with fresh spinach, nutty Parmesan cheese, and a little zest from the crushed red pepper—is a good source of protein, carbs, and iron.

● ○ ○ **Easy**

PREP 10 mins
COOK about 21 mins

YIELD 4 servings

INGREDIENTS

1 cup orzo pasta

2 TB. extra-virgin olive oil

2 cloves garlic, minced

¼ tsp. crushed red pepper flakes

2 (16-oz.; 450g) boneless, skinless chicken breasts, cut into 1-in. (2.5cm) cubes

½ tsp. salt

½ tsp. freshly cracked black pepper

1 TB. fresh parsley, chopped

2 cups fresh baby spinach

½ cup grated Parmesan cheese

For a vegetarian version, use 1 pound (450g) extra-firm tofu, cut into ½-inch (1.25cm) cubes. Add tofu at the same time the chicken would have been added, and continue recipe as directed.

For a gluten-free dish, use gluten-free pasta instead of the orzo.

1 Fill a large pot with water, set over medium-high heat, and bring to a boil. Add orzo pasta, and cook for 8 to 10 minutes or until al dente. Drain.

2 In a medium skillet over medium-high heat, heat extra-virgin olive oil. Add garlic and crushed red pepper flakes, and cook for about 1 minute or until garlic is lightly golden.

3 Stir in chicken, salt, and black pepper, and cook for 2 to 5 minutes or until lightly browned and chicken is cooked through.

4 Reduce heat to medium, and mix in parsley and cooked pasta. Add baby spinach, and continue cooking, stirring occasionally, for about 5 minutes or until spinach is wilted.

5 Stir in Parmesan cheese, and serve hot.

Storage: Refrigerate leftovers for 3 to 5 days.

NUTRITION PER SERVING			
CALORIES	420	FAT	14g
CARBOHYDRATES	39g	CHOLESTEROL	80mg
SUGARS	2g	SODIUM	600mg
DIETARY FIBER	2g	VITAMIN C	8%
PROTEIN	35g	VITAMIN A	15%
		IRON	15%

Slow Cooked **Corned Beef and Cabbage**

Corned beef and cabbage has never been easier. This version has a ton of protein and carbs to fuel your body and is an excellent source of vitamins A and C.

● ● ○ **Intermediate**

PREP 15 mins
COOK 6 hours

YIELD 8 servings

INGREDIENTS

3 lb. (1.5kg) corned beef brisket
  with spice packet

1 small head cabbage,
  cut into wedges

4 medium carrots, peeled and
  cut into 2-in. (5cm) pieces

1 medium yellow onion,
  cut into wedges

18 fingerling potatoes

½ cup water

1 Cut corned beef brisket to fit into a 5- or 6-quart (4.75 to 5.5l) slow cooker. Evenly sprinkle spice packet over brisket, and rub in with your fingers.

2 Add cabbage, carrots, yellow onion, and fingerling potatoes to the slow cooker.

3 Pour water over vegetables, and top with brisket.

4 Cover and cook on high for 6 hours or until meat is fork-tender.

5 Remove brisket from the slow cooker, slice into 8 servings, and serve hot with vegetables.

Storage: Refrigerate leftovers for 3 to 5 days.

To lower the fat in this recipe, trim off any excess fat from the beef brisket before cooking. And to decrease the sodium some, use less of the seasoning packet that comes with the corned beef brisket.

NUTRITION PER SERVING			
CALORIES	650	FAT	26g
CARBOHYDRATES	70g	CHOLESTEROL	90mg
SUGARS	9g	SODIUM	2,150mg
DIETARY FIBER	9g	VITAMIN C	200%
PROTEIN	34g	VITAMIN A	100%
		IRON	30%

Spaghetti with **Meat Sauce**

This simple and classic dish is full of carbs and protein to help you recover after a hard workout.

1 In a large saucepan over medium-high heat, combine beef, yellow onion, garlic, and green bell pepper. Cook, stirring occasionally, for about 5 minutes or until meat is browned and vegetables are tender. Drain off grease.

2 Stir in diced tomatoes, crushed tomatoes, and tomato paste. Season with oregano, basil, salt, and black pepper. Simmer spaghetti sauce, stirring occasionally, for 1 hour.

3 When spaghetti sauce is about 10 minutes from being done, fill a large pot with water, and set over medium-high heat. Bring water to a boil, and cook spaghetti noodles, stirring occasionally, for about 8 minutes or until al dente.

4 Evenly divide spaghetti and sauce among 8 plates or bowls, and serve hot immediately.

Make ahead: Prepare meat sauce up to 3 to 5 days ahead and refrigerate, or freeze for up to 2 months.

To make this a slow-cooker recipe, complete step 1 as directed and then add all ingredients (except for the pasta) to a 5-quart (4.75l) slow cooker. Cover, and cook on low for 6 to 8 hours. Cook the pasta when the sauce is just about finished cooking, and serve as directed.

● ○ ○ **Easy**

PREP 15 mins
COOK 1 hour, 13 mins

YIELD 8 servings

INGREDIENTS

1 lb. (450g) 90% lean ground beef

1 small yellow onion, chopped

4 cloves garlic, minced

1 small green bell pepper, ribs and seeds removed, and diced

1 (28-oz.; 800g) can diced tomatoes, with juice

1 (16-oz.; 450g) can crushed tomatoes, with juice

1 (6-oz.; 170g) can tomato paste

2 tsp. dried oregano

2 tsp. dried basil

1 tsp. salt

½ tsp. freshly cracked black pepper

1 lb. (450g) spaghetti noodles

For a gluten-free version, use gluten-free pasta instead of the spaghetti.

NUTRITION PER SERVING			
CALORIES	380	FAT	7g
CARBOHYDRATES	55g	CHOLESTEROL	35mg
SUGARS	10g	SODIUM	860mg
DIETARY FIBER	4g	VITAMIN C	60%
PROTEIN	21g	VITAMIN A	20%
		IRON	20%

Spaghetti with Turkey Pesto
Meatballs

This quick and simple meal is loaded with carbs and full of lean protein, thanks to the turkey meatballs.

1 Spread 1 cup tomato pasta sauce in the bottom of a medium, heavy skillet.

2 In a medium bowl, combine turkey, breadcrumbs, pesto sauce, egg white, garlic, and salt. Using moistened hands, form mixture into 4 medium meatballs.

3 Place meatballs in single layer in the skillet, and spoon remaining pasta sauce over top.

4 Set the skillet over medium heat, and bring to a simmer. Cover, reduce heat to medium-low, and simmer, stirring occasionally, for about 25 to 30 minutes or until meatballs are cooked through.

5 Meanwhile, fill a large pot with water, and set over medium-high heat. Bring water to a boil, add spaghetti noodles, and cook for about 10 minutes or until just tender but still firm to bite.

6 Drain pasta and divide between 2 bowls. Top with meatballs and sauce, and serve hot.

Make ahead and freeze: Prepare up to end of step 3 up to 3 days ahead. Freeze after step 3 for up to 2 months. Thaw in refrigerator for 4 or 5 hours before baking.

 Intermediate

PREP 15 to 20 mins
COOK about 40 mins

YIELD 2 servings

INGREDIENTS

2 cups chunky tomato pasta sauce

½ lb. (225g) ground turkey

½ cup dry unseasoned breadcrumbs

2¾ TB. pesto sauce

1 large egg white

1 tsp. fresh minced garlic

¼ tsp. salt

8 oz. (225g) spaghetti noodles

NUTRITION PER SERVING			
CALORIES	810	FAT	15g
CARBOHYDRATES	117g	CHOLESTEROL	50mg
SUGARS	13g	SODIUM	1,540mg
DIETARY FIBER	6g	VITAMIN C	60%
PROTEIN	55g	VITAMIN A	30%
		IRON	35%

To lower the fat of the recipe even more, use ground turkey breast instead of ground turkey. Ground turkey can often include other parts of the turkey, such as the skin, which is higher in fat.

Blackened **Tilapia**

Tender whitefish is rubbed with zesty spices and blackened to perfection in this delicious, low-fiber main dish for recovery meals.

1 Preheat the oven to 425°F (220°C). Line a baking sheet with parchment paper.

2 In a small bowl, combine paprika, salt, onion powder, black pepper, cayenne, thyme, oregano, and garlic powder.

3 Rinse and pat dry tilapia fillets, brush with extra-virgin olive oil, and completely coat with seasoning mixture. Place tilapia on the prepared baking sheet, and spray tilapia lightly with cooking spray.

4 Bake tilapia for about 15 to 20 minutes or until golden brown and cooked through.

5 Serve immediately.

Storage: Refrigerate leftovers for 3 to 5 days.

To make this recipe vegetarian, substitute 4 (4-ounce; 110g) portions of extra-firm tofu, drained and coated with seasonings as you would the tilapia. Prepare the same way.

 ● ● ● **Easy**

PREP 8 mins
COOK 11 mins

YIELD 4 servings

INGREDIENTS

3 TB. paprika

1 tsp. salt

1 TB. onion powder

1 tsp. freshly cracked black pepper

½ tsp. cayenne

1 tsp. dried thyme

1 tsp. dried oregano

1 tsp. garlic powder

1 lb. (450g) tilapia fillets

1 TB. extra-virgin olive oil

Cooking spray

NUTRITION PER SERVING

CALORIES	150	FAT	6g
CARBOHYDRATES	3g	CHOLESTEROL	55mg
SUGARS	0g	SODIUM	640mg
DIETARY FIBER	2g	VITAMIN C	6%
PROTEIN	23g	VITAMIN A	50%
		IRON	10%

Reserve any leftover seasoning—that didn't come in contact with the fish—and use it when cooking beef, chicken, or even pork.

Shrimp **Scampi**

This high-protein shrimp favorite features zesty garlic, a little sweetness from white wine, spice from black pepper and crushed red pepper flakes, and a splash of citrus.

  ● ● ○ **Intermediate**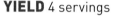

PREP 10 mins
COOK 5 mins

YIELD 4 servings

INGREDIENTS

2 TB. salted butter

2 TB. extra-virgin olive oil

4 cloves garlic, sliced

¼ tsp. crushed red pepper flakes

1 lb. (450g) shrimp (16 to 20 count), shelled and deveined

½ cup white wine

2 TB. fresh parsley, chopped

¼ tsp. freshly cracked black pepper

Juice of ½ medium lemon (1 TB.)

1 In a large skillet over medium heat, heat salted butter and extra-virgin olive oil until butter is melted. Add garlic and crushed red pepper flakes, and sauté for 1 minute or until garlic begins to lightly brown.

2 Add shrimp and white wine, increase heat to high, and cook for 2 or 3 minutes. Flip over shrimp, and cook other side for 1 minute. Remove the pan from heat.

3 Sprinkle parsley and black pepper over shrimp, and drizzle lemon juice over top. Toss to combine, and serve hot.

Storage: Refrigerate leftovers for 3 to 5 days.

This is a great recipe to serve as a main dish with a number of different sides. To turn it into an easy meal, serve with pasta. Choose gluten-free pasta or rice to make it a gluten-free meal.

NUTRITION PER SERVING			
CALORIES	260	FAT	14g
CARBOHYDRATES	2g	CHOLESTEROL	235mg
SUGARS	0g	SODIUM	300mg
DIETARY FIBER	0g	VITAMIN C	8%
PROTEIN	24g	VITAMIN A	10%
		IRON	20%

Buffalo Chicken **Pizza**

Make this sensational pizza, packed with tons of flavor from the zesty buffalo sauce and tangy blue cheese, any night of the week.

1 Preheat the oven to 350°F (150°C).

2 Place pizza crust on a baking stone or baking sheet. Spread buffalo-style hot sauce over crust, and layer chicken, mozzarella cheese, and blue cheese on top.

3 Bake on the baking stone or sheet for 20 to 25 minutes or until cheese has melted and is bubbly.

Make ahead and freeze: Prepare up to end of step 2 up to 3 days ahead. Freeze after step 3 for up to 2 months. Bake from frozen.

 ● ○ ○ **Easy**

PREP 5 mins
COOK 25 mins

YIELD 8 servings

INGREDIENTS

1 (16-oz.; 450g) pkg. original-style prebaked pizza crust

½ cup buffalo-style hot sauce

2 cups cooked chicken breast, diced

1 cup shredded reduced-fat mozzarella cheese

¼ cup crumbled blue cheese

NUTRITION PER SERVING

CALORIES	270	FAT	8g
CARBOHYDRATES	29g	CHOLESTEROL	30mg
SUGARS	1g	SODIUM	1,090mg
DIETARY FIBER	2g	VITAMIN C	0%
PROTEIN	18g	VITAMIN A	4%
		IRON	10%

To make this recipe gluten free, choose a gluten-free pizza crust. To make it vegetarian, substitute firm tofu, crumbled, or seitan for the chicken breast.

Sweet and Salty
Bacon-Wrapped Asparagus

Crisp bacon wrapped around fresh asparagus with a sweet and salty glaze makes a delicious side to your favorite recovery entrée—or a light meal by itself.

● ● ○ **Intermediate**

PREP 10 to 15 mins
COOK about 35 mins

YIELD 12 servings

INGREDIENTS

2 lb. (1kg) fresh asparagus spears, ends trimmed

12 slices raw bacon

½ cup light brown sugar, packed

¼ cup unsalted butter

1 TB. low-sodium soy sauce

½ tsp. garlic powder

¼ tsp. freshly cracked black pepper

1 Preheat the oven to 400°F (200°C).

2 Divide asparagus into 12 bundles, about 3 or 4 spears in each bundle.

3 Wrap 1 piece of bacon around each asparagus bundle, secure bacon to asparagus with a toothpick, and place in a shallow baking pan.

4 In a small saucepan over low heat, combine light brown sugar, butter, soy sauce, garlic powder, and black pepper. Cook, stirring occasionally, for 3 to 5 minutes or until butter is melted. Pour mixture over asparagus bundles.

5 Bake for 25 to 30 minutes or until bacon is fully cooked.

6 Serve hot or at room temperature.

NUTRITION PER SERVING			
CALORIES	190	FAT	14g
CARBOHYDRATES	12g	CHOLESTEROL	25mg
SUGARS	10g	SODIUM	230mg
DIETARY FIBER	2g	VITAMIN C	8%
PROTEIN	4g	VITAMIN A	15%
		IRON	10%

Roasted **Butternut Squash**

Sweet butternut squash, simply seasoned and oven-roasted, is a savory side to warm you on a cold day.

1 Preheat the oven to 400°F (200°C).

2 In a large bowl, toss butternut squash with extra-virgin olive oil, garlic, salt, and black pepper. Spread squash onto a baking sheet.

3 Roast for about 25 to 30 minutes or until squash is tender and lightly browned.

4 Serve hot immediately.

Storage: Refrigerate leftovers for 3 to 5 days.

● ○ ○ **Easy**

PREP 15 mins
COOK about 25 to 30 mins

YIELD 4 servings

INGREDIENTS

1 (2– or 3-lb.; 1 to 1.5kg) butternut squash, peeled, seeded, and cut into 1-in. (2.5cm) cubes

2 TB. extra-virgin olive oil

2 cloves fresh garlic, minced

1 tsp. salt

½ tsp. freshly cracked black pepper

For a quick butternut squash soup, blend all the ingredients in a blender for 2 or 3 minutes with about 2 cups 2% milk and 2 tablespoons honey. Add blended butternut squash mixture to a medium pot over medium-low heat, and cook, stirring occasionally, for about 5 minutes or until heated through. Adjust seasoning as needed, and serve hot.

NUTRITION PER SERVING			
CALORIES	190	FAT	7g
CARBOHYDRATES	34g	CHOLESTEROL	0mg
SUGARS	6g	SODIUM	590mg
DIETARY FIBER	6g	VITAMIN C	100%
PROTEIN	3g	VITAMIN A	610%
		IRON	10%

Reduced-Fat **Creamed Spinach**

This comfort-food side has all the flavor of traditional creamed spinach but is much lower in fat and calories.

● ● ● **Intermediate**

PREP 5 to 10 mins
COOK about 12 mins

YIELD 6 servings

INGREDIENTS

1 TB. plus 2 tsp. extra-virgin olive oil

2 (16-oz.; 450g) bags fresh baby spinach

1 tsp. salt

½ tsp. freshly cracked black pepper

⅛ tsp. cayenne

⅛ tsp. ground nutmeg

2 TB. minced shallots

¾ cup 2% milk

1 tsp. lemon zest, freshly grated

2 TB. grated Parmesan cheese

1 In a large pot over medium heat, heat 2 teaspoons extra-virgin olive oil. Add baby spinach, cover, and cook for about 1 minute. Uncover, and stir until all spinach leaves are wilted.

2 Drain spinach in a strainer, and transfer to a paper towel–lined plate. When spinach is cool enough to handle, squeeze out as much liquid as possible, transfer spinach to a cutting board, and roughly chop.

3 In a small bowl, combine salt, black pepper, cayenne, and nutmeg.

4 In the same large pot over medium heat, heat remaining 1 tablespoon extra-virgin olive oil. Add shallots, stir, and cook for about 3 or 4 minutes or until just golden brown.

5 Stir in seasoning mixture and 2% milk, and cook for about 5 minutes or until milk is reduced by about half.

6 Stir in lemon zest.

7 Reduce heat to low, add spinach, and cook, stirring, for about 2 minutes or until spinach is heated through and coated with sauce.

8 Stir in Parmesan cheese, and serve hot immediately.

Storage: Refrigerate leftovers for 3 to 5 days.

NUTRITION PER SERVING			
CALORIES	120	FAT	5g
CARBOHYDRATES	18g	CHOLESTEROL	5mg
SUGARS	2g	SODIUM	670mg
DIETARY FIBER	7g	VITAMIN C	35%
PROTEIN	5g	VITAMIN A	110%
		IRON	25%

Orange **Creamcicles**

These cool and creamy pops are a delicious and refreshing treat after a hot summer workout!

● ○ ○ **Easy**

PREP 5 mins + freeze time

YIELD 10 servings

INGREDIENTS

2 cups vanilla Greek yogurt

1 (12-oz.; 350ml) can frozen
   orange juice concentrate

¼ tsp. salt

1 In a small bowl, combine vanilla yogurt, orange juice concentrate, and salt.

2 Evenly divide yogurt mixture among 10 ice pop molds, and freeze overnight.

Storage: Freeze leftovers for up to 1 week.

NUTRITION PER SERVING			
CALORIES	100	FAT	0g
CARBOHYDRATES	22g	CHOLESTEROL	5mg
SUGARS	20g	SODIUM	80mg
DIETARY FIBER	0g	VITAMIN C	60%
PROTEIN	2g	VITAMIN A	4%
		IRON	0%

Super-Easy **Key Lime Pie**

This is a light and airy take on the classic Key lime pie, using lime gelatin, reduced-fat whipped topping, and yogurt.

1 In a large bowl, dissolve lime gelatin in boiling water.

2 Whisk in Key lime yogurt, fold in whipped topping, and pour filling into graham cracker piecrust.

3 Cover and refrigerate for at least 2 hours or until set.

4 Serve chilled.

Make ahead and freeze: Prepare up to end of step 4 up to 3 days ahead. Freeze after step 4 for up to 2 months.

Storage: Refrigerate leftovers for 3 to 5 days.

 Easy

PREP 20 mins + 2 hours chill time

YIELD 8 servings

INGREDIENTS

1 (.3-oz.; 8.5g) pkg. lime gelatin

¼ cup boiling water

2 (6-oz; 170g) pkg. Key lime yogurt

1 (8-oz.; 225g) pkg. reduced-fat whipped topping, thawed

1 (9-in.; 23cm) graham cracker piecrust

NUTRITION PER SERVING			
CALORIES	260	FAT	11g
CARBOHYDRATES	38g	CHOLESTEROL	5mg
SUGARS	22g	SODIUM	200mg
DIETARY FIBER	0g	VITAMIN C	0%
PROTEIN	3g	VITAMIN A	8%
		IRON	4%

For a lighter twist on a classic lemon meringue pie, use lemon meringue yogurt (or just lemon) and lemon juice in place of the lime. And to make this recipe gluten free, simply use a gluten-free graham cracker piecrust.

Strawberry **Pie**

This delicious and easy-to-prepare classic summer pie features fresh strawberries and plenty of carbs to help your body recover after a strenuous workout.

● ● ◐ **Intermediate**

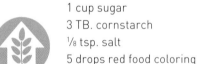

PREP 4 hours, 15 mins +
3 hours chill time
COOK 20 to 25 mins

YIELD 8 servings

INGREDIENTS

1 (9-in.; 23cm) premade piecrust

6 cups fresh strawberries, hulled and sliced

1 cup sugar

3 TB. cornstarch

1/8 tsp. salt

5 drops red food coloring

1   Preheat the oven to 450°F (230°C).

2   Bake piecrust for 8 to 10 minutes or until lightly browned. Remove from the oven, and cool completely on a wire rack (about 15 minutes).

3   Meanwhile, in a small bowl, crush enough strawberries to make 1 cup.

4   In a 2-quart (2l) saucepan over medium heat, combine sugar, cornstarch, and salt, and stir in crushed strawberries. Cook, stirring constantly, for 5 to 10 minutes or until mixture boils and thickens.

5   Mix in red food coloring. Remove the pan from heat, and allow to cool completely (about 30 minutes).

6   Place remaining strawberries in cooled piecrust, pour cooled strawberry mixture evenly over berries, and refrigerate for about 3 hours or until set.

7   Serve chilled.

Storage: Refrigerate leftovers for 3 to 5 days.

To make this recipe gluten free, opt for a gluten-free piecrust.

NUTRITION PER SERVING			
CALORIES	230	FAT	6g
CARBOHYDRATES	48g	CHOLESTEROL	0mg
SUGARS	19g	SODIUM	160mg
DIETARY FIBER	6g	VITAMIN C	60%
PROTEIN	2g	VITAMIN A	2%
		IRON	4%

Black Bean **Brownies**

You won't believe how deliciously fudgy these brownies are! Using black beans instead of oil and eggs reduces the fat and boosts the protein.

● ○ ○ ○ **Easy**

PREP 5 mins
COOK 50 mins

YIELD 16 servings

INGREDIENTS

1 (15-oz.; 420g) can black beans, drained and rinsed
1 box dark chocolate brownie mix

1 Preheat the oven to 375°F (190°C). Lightly grease a 8×8-inch (20×20cm) baking pan.

2 After draining and rinsing black beans in the can, fill the can with water (with beans still inside). Pour beans and water into a blender, and purée until smooth.

3 In a large bowl, stir together dark chocolate brownie mix and puréed beans until completely combined. Pour batter into the prepared baking pan and smooth batter evenly.

4 Bake for about 50 minutes or until a toothpick inserted into the center comes out clean.

5 Cool brownies completely before cutting into 16 squares.

Make ahead and freeze: Prepare brownie mix up to end of step 3 up to 3 days ahead. Refrigerate after step 5 for up to 5 days, or freeze for up to 2 months.

Storage: Refrigerate leftovers for 3 to 5 days.

For different flavor options, mix in ½ cup of your favorite dried fruits or chopped nuts. And to make this recipe gluten free, use a gluten-free brownie mix.

NUTRITION PER SERVING			
CALORIES	130	FAT	2g
CARBOHYDRATES	27g	CHOLESTEROL	0mg
SUGARS	16g	SODIUM	180mg
DIETARY FIBER	2g	VITAMIN C	0%
PROTEIN	2g	VITAMIN A	0%
		IRON	6%

Meal **Plans**

In this appendix, we share meal plans, one for endurance athletes and one for strength athletes. Both have been prepared for an athlete who weighs 180 pounds (82kg), and workout/competition times for this athlete are in the afternoon. Use these menus as a guideline for how you could set up your own so you're sure to consume enough nutrition and meet your body's needs.

ENDURANCE ATHLETES

See "Determining Your Caloric and Nutrient Needs" for guidance in adapting this meal plan to your situation.

Nutrition based on a 180-pound (82kg) athlete.

DAILY NUTRITION

Calories: 3,000

Fat: 80 to 90 grams

Carbohydrates: 500 to 600 grams

Protein: 90 to 110 grams

Meal/Snack	Timing	Menu Item	Nutrition
Breakfast		1 serving Quickie Breakfast Burritos 8 ounces (225g) low-fat milk 1 medium banana 1 cup 100% fruit juice	507 calories 11g fat 84g carbohydrates 22g protein
Morning snack		1 cup sliced strawberries and 1 cup fresh blueberries 1 serving Low-Fat Banana Bread 1 cup 100% fruit juice	364 calories 4g fat 81g carbohydrates 7g protein
Lunch	3 or 4 hours before training/competition	1 serving Whole-Wheat Turkey and Veggie Pita Sandwich 1 serving Quick Tortellini Salad 1 medium apple 8 ounces (225g) low-fat chocolate milk 1 cup 100% fruit juice	809 calories 21g fat 135g carbohydrates 31g protein
Afternoon snack	1 hour before training/competition	10 hard pretzel twists 1 cup grapes	289 calories 2g fat 64g carbohydrates 7g protein
Training/ competition	During training/ competition	1 serving Snack Mix Cereal Bars 1 serving Mango Cooler	410 calories 12g fat 72g carbohydrates 7g protein
Dinner	30 minutes to 1 hour after training/competition	1 serving Easy Slow Cooker Pot Roast 1 cup white rice ½ cup mixed vegetables 1 cup 100% fruit juice	677 calories 18g fat 81g carbohydrates 32g protein
Evening snack		1 cup orange sherbet	260 calories 4g fat 54g carbohydrates 2g protein

TOTAL NUTRITION BREAKDOWN

Calories: 3,316

Fat: 72 grams

Carbohydrates: 499 grams

Protein: 108 grams

ADAPTING PLANS

To adjust the sample menus, determine your caloric needs, and add or subtract calories (and the associated menu items) to fit your needs. Make substitutions for snacks or entrées as needed.

If you have a workout/competition in the morning, rearrange the sample menu as appropriate to the time when you have your workout/competition and use the timing guidelines as recommended.

STRENGTH ATHLETES

See "Determining Your Caloric and Nutrient Needs" for guidance in adapting this meal plan to your situation.

Nutrition based on a 180-pound (82kg) athlete.

DAILY NUTRITION:

Calories: 3,000

Fat: 70 to 80 grams

Carbohydrates:
400 to 500 grams

Protein: 120 to 140 grams

Meal/Snack	Timing	Menu Item	Nutrition
Breakfast		1 cup cooked oatmeal (add 2 tablespoons brown sugar, 1 tablespoon sliced almonds, and ¼ cup fresh blueberries) 8 ounces (225g) low-fat milk 1 medium banana	399 calories 16g fat 66g carbohydrates 13g protein
Morning snack		8 ounces (225g) low-fat yogurt 1 Sweet and Salty Peanut Bar 1 cup grapes	524 calories 15g fat 101g carbohydrates 23g protein
Lunch	3 or 4 hours before training/competition	1 serving Shrimp and Spinach Pasta 1 medium apple 1 cup 100% fruit juice	766 calories 11g fat 106g carbohydrates 39g protein
Afternoon snack	1 hour before training/competition	1 serving Acai Punch 1 medium apple	169 calories 0g fat 42g carbohydrates 0g protein
Training/ competition	During training/ competition	1 serving Blueberry Madness Bars 1 serving Blackberry Cooler	370 calories 16g fat 52g carbohydrates 4g protein
Dinner	30 minutes to 1 hour after training/competition	1 serving Beef, Broccoli, and Yam Stir-Fry 1½ cups white rice 1 cup 100% fruit juice	796 calories 19g fat 103g carbohydrates 34g protein
Evening snack		1 serving Lavender Lemonade Relaxer 1 cup sliced strawberries with ¼ cup low-fat whipped topping	245 calories 2g fat 71g carbohydrate 1g protein

TOTAL NUTRITION BREAKDOWN

Calories: 3,269

Fat: 79 grams

Carbohydrates: 541 grams

Protein: 118 grams

Common **Conversions**

All recipes in this book give U.S. standard and Imperial measurements with metric equivalents for liquid and dry ingredients as well as temperatures. Use these tables for further reference or for converting the measures and temperatures in other cookbooks.

LIQUID MEASUREMENTS

U.S. Standard	Imperial	Metric
¼ teaspoon	—	.75 milliliter
½ teaspoon	—	1.25 milliliters
1 teaspoon	—	2.5 milliliters
½ tablespoon (1½ teaspoons)	—	3.75 milliliters
1 tablespoon (3 teaspoons)	½ fluid ounce	7.5 milliliters
⅛ cup (2 tablespoons)	1 fluid ounce	30 milliliters
¼ cup (4 tablespoons)	2 fluid ounces	55 milliliters
⅓ cup (5 tablespoons)	2½ fluid ounces	62.5 milliliters
½ cup (8 tablespoons)	4 fluid ounces	110 milliliters
⅔ cup (10 tablespoons)	5 fluid ounces	140 milliliters
¾ cup (12 tablespoons)	6 fluid ounces	170 milliliters
1 cup (16 tablespoons)	8 fluid ounces (½ pint)	240 milliliters
2 cups	16 fluid ounces (1 pint)	480 milliliters
4 cups	32 fluid ounces (1 quart)	960 milliliters
4 quarts	128 fluid ounces (1 gallon)	4 liters

DRY MEASURING CUPS
A good set of measuring cups is essential for accurate cooking.

DRY MEASURES

U.S. Standard	Metric
1 ounce	25 grams
2 ounces	55 grams
4 ounces (¼ pound)	110 grams
5 ounces (⅓ pound)	140 grams
6 ounces	170 grams
7 ounces	200 grams
8 ounces (½ pound)	225 grams
10 ounces (⅔ pound)	285 grams
12 ounces (¾ pound)	340 grams
14 ounces	400 grams
15 ounces	420 grams
16 ounces (1 pound)	450 grams
32 ounces (2 pounds)	950 grams

TEMPERATURES

Degrees Fahrenheit	Degrees Celsius
225	110
250	120
275	140
300	150
325	170
350	180
375	190
400	200
425	220
450	230

KITCHEN SCALE
Measuring ingredients by weight is more accurate than by volume, but not everyone owns a scale.

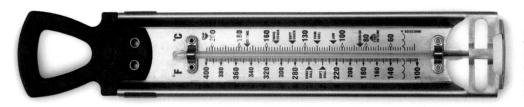

KITCHEN THERMOMETER
Use a kitchen thermometer to ensure meats are cooked to a safe temperature.

Calculating **BMI** and **Body Fat Percentage**

In this appendix, we share a few tools to help you assess how your body weight and body composition can impact your overall health. You can use these tools to help you get to a healthy weight; they also provide good information about your overall health status and risk for heart disease, diabetes, or stroke. BMI (body mass index) and body fat percentage are currently two of the most common, quick, and inexpensive tools used to assess body fat and overall health status.

BMI

BMI estimates the amount of body fat a person has and typically correlates with being overweight or obese. Weight gain is associated with an increase in BMI, which also increases your risk of developing long-term chronic diseases.

BMI does have its drawbacks. It doesn't distinguish fat from muscle. For example, a body builder could have a BMI in the obese category yet actually have a normal to low body fat percentage. Also, two individuals at the same height and weight might have the same BMI yet have totally different body compositions and body fat percentages.

Professional athletes, especially body builders, may benefit from additional forms of body composition assessment such as skinfold measurements and body fat percentage to provide a better indication of lean body mass versus fat mass.

BODY MASS INDEX

	Normal						Overweight					Obese									
BMI	19	20	21	22	23	24	25	26	27	28	29	30	31	32	33	34	35	36	37	38	39
Height (inches)														Body Weight (pounds)							
58	91	96	100	105	110	115	119	124	129	134	138	143	148	153	158	162	167	172	177	181	186
59	94	99	104	109	114	119	124	128	133	138	143	148	153	158	163	168	173	178	183	188	193
60	97	102	107	112	118	123	128	133	138	143	148	153	158	163	168	174	179	184	189	194	199
61	100	106	111	116	122	127	132	137	143	148	153	158	164	169	174	180	185	190	195	201	206
62	104	109	115	120	126	131	136	142	147	153	158	164	169	175	180	186	191	196	202	207	213
63	107	113	118	124	130	135	141	146	152	158	163	169	175	180	186	191	197	203	208	214	220
64	110	116	122	128	134	140	145	151	157	163	169	174	180	186	192	197	204	209	215	221	227
65	114	120	126	132	138	144	150	156	162	168	174	180	186	192	198	204	210	216	222	228	234
66	118	124	130	136	142	148	155	161	167	173	179	186	192	198	204	210	216	223	229	235	241
67	121	127	134	140	146	153	159	166	172	178	185	191	198	204	211	217	223	230	236	242	249
68	125	131	138	144	151	158	164	171	177	184	190	197	203	210	216	223	230	236	243	249	256
69	128	135	142	149	155	162	169	176	182	189	196	203	209	216	223	230	236	243	250	257	263
70	132	139	146	153	160	167	174	181	188	195	202	209	216	222	229	236	243	250	257	264	271
71	136	143	150	157	165	172	179	186	193	200	208	215	222	229	236	243	250	257	265	272	279
72	140	147	154	162	169	177	184	191	199	206	213	221	228	235	242	250	258	265	272	279	287
73	144	151	159	166	174	182	189	197	204	212	219	227	235	242	250	257	265	272	280	288	295
74	148	155	163	171	179	186	194	202	210	218	225	233	241	249	256	264	272	280	287	295	303
75	152	160	168	176	184	192	200	208	216	224	232	240	248	256	264	272	279	287	295	303	311
76	156	164	172	180	189	197	205	213	221	230	238	246	254	263	271	279	287	295	304	312	320

Source: National Heart, Lung, and Blood Institute, National Institutes of Health

BODY FAT PERCENTAGE

Body fat percentage is the total mass of fat divided by the total body mass. Body fat percentage is unique in that it doesn't use height or weight as factors; it strictly evaluates body composition. There are two ways you can determine your body fat percentage.

The first uses skinfold calipers to measure the fat at several standardized areas on your body. These measurements can be used to estimate your overall body fat percentage.

The second method uses a bioelectrical impedance device that sends electrical signals through your body to determine your body fat percentage. Muscle is a better conductor of electricity because it contains a large amount of water as opposed to fat, which is a poor conductor of electricity. The device uses this difference to determine the percentage of fat versus muscle.

BODY FAT RANGES

Classification	Men	Women
Athlete	6 to 13%	14 to 20%
Physically fit	14 to 17%	21 to 24%
Average	18 to 24%	25 to 31%
Overweight/obese	25% and greater	32% and greater

Source: American Council on Exercise

The caliper method yields a more accurate result but depends on the skill of the person taking the measurements. Ask a trainer at your local gym to help you determine yours.

The preceding table provides ranges for various body fat percentage categories for men and women. (A higher range of body fat is normal for women versus men.)

Extreme Obesity

40	41	42	43	44	45	46	47	48	49	50	51	52	53	54
191	196	201	205	210	215	220	224	229	234	239	244	248	253	258
198	203	208	212	217	222	227	232	237	242	247	252	257	262	267
204	209	215	220	225	230	235	240	245	250	255	261	266	271	276
211	217	222	227	232	238	243	248	254	259	264	269	275	280	285
218	224	229	235	240	246	251	256	262	267	273	278	284	289	295
225	231	237	242	248	254	259	265	270	278	282	287	293	299	304
232	238	244	250	256	262	267	273	279	285	291	296	302	308	314
240	246	252	258	264	270	276	282	288	294	300	306	312	318	324
247	253	260	266	272	278	284	291	297	303	309	315	322	328	334
255	261	268	274	280	287	293	299	306	312	319	325	331	338	344
262	269	276	282	289	295	302	308	315	322	328	335	341	348	354
270	277	284	291	297	304	311	318	324	331	338	345	351	358	365
278	285	292	299	306	313	320	327	334	341	348	355	362	369	376
286	293	301	308	315	322	329	338	343	351	358	365	372	379	386
294	302	309	316	324	331	338	346	353	361	368	375	383	390	397
302	310	318	325	333	340	348	355	363	371	378	386	393	401	408
311	319	326	334	342	350	358	365	373	381	389	396	404	412	420
319	327	335	343	351	359	367	375	383	391	399	407	415	423	431
328	336	344	353	361	369	377	385	394	402	410	418	426	435	443

Recipes by **Nutrient Content**

 ## High Carb

Provides important fuel for endurance activities.

High Fiber

Ideal for larger meals 3 to 5 hours before activity.

 # High Protein

Gives fuel for strength and rebuilding muscle.

Baked Egg and Tomato Cups, **122–123**

Banana Orange Sunrise Smoothie, **112–113**

Basil Penne Pasta with Asparagus and Feta, **184**

Beef, Broccoli, and Yam Stir-Fry, **94–95**

Blackened Tilapia, **194–195**

Blueberry Orange Parfaits, **100–101**

Buffalo Chicken Pizza, **198–199**

Carb-Loaded Bean and Vegetable Soup, **74–75**

Cherries Jubilee Bars, **167**

Chickpea, Tomato, and Mozzarella Salad with Pesto, **180–181**

Chickpea, Tomato, and Pasta Soup, **130–131**

Chickpea Salad, **80**

Chocolate Peanut Butter Bars, **166**

Classic Chef Salad, **80**

Coffeecake Power Muffins, **66–67**

Country Frittata, **120–121**

Easy Italian Pasta Salad, **138**

Easy Minestrone Soup, **132–133**

Easy Slow Cooker Pot Roast, **139**

Egg Drop Soup, **134**

Fantastic Fudge Pops, **144–145**

Garlic Chicken with Orzo Pasta, **188–189**

Greek Pasta Salad, **78–79**

Green Monster Smoothie, **114–115**

Hearty Legume Soup, **170**

Homemade Hamburger Casserole, **142–143**

Italian Wedding Soup, **135**

Lean Steak and Brown Rice Stir-Fry, **185**

Lentil Soup, **76**

Marinated Greek Orzo Salad, **178–179**

Maryland Vegetable Crab Soup, **77**

Mediterranean Quinoa Salad, **174–175**

Mediterranean Salmon Wraps, **158–159**

Mixed Berry Blenderita Smoothie, **112–113**

Peaches and Cream Smoothie, **114–115**

Power-Packed Cauliflower Tacos, **90–91**

Quickie Breakfast Burrito, **124–125**

Reduced-Fat Tuna Melts, **156–157**

Seafood Chowder, **172–173**

Shrimp and Spinach Pasta, **93**

Shrimp Scampi, **196–197**

Simple Chicken Marsala, **140–141**

Slow Cooker Corned Beef and Cabbage, **190**

Snack Mix Cereal Bars, **118–119**

Spaghetti with Meat Sauce, **191**

Spaghetti with Turkey Pesto Meatballs, **192–193**

Strawberry Shortcake Milkshakes, **96–97**

Stuffed Zucchini Boats, **84–85**

Sun-Dried Tomato and Feta Omelet, **82–83**

Super-Simple Couscous Salad, **176–177**

Sweet and Salty Peanut Bars, **62**

Teriyaki Salmon, **88–89**

Three Cheese and Spinach Stuffed Shells, **92**

Tropical Island Snack Mix, **63**

Turkey and Scallion Wraps, **128–129**

Turkey Chili, **171**

Vegetable Stew, **168–169**

White Beans and Broccoli, **182–183**

Whole-Wheat Oatmeal Pancakes, **86–87**

Whole-Wheat Turkey and Veggie Pita Sandwich, **60–61**

Zucchini Pizza Casserole, **186–187**

 # Low Fat

Keeps calories down to avoid weight gain and promote cardiovascular health.

Acai Punch, **54**

Baked Country Ham, Egg, and Cheese Cups, **56–57**

Banana Orange Sunrise Smoothie, **112–113**

Black Bean Brownies, **210–211**

Blackberry Cooler, **54**

Blackened Tilapia, **194–195**

Blueberry Banana Recovery Smoothie, **154–155**

Blueberry Lavender Lemonade, **152**

Carb-Loaded Bean and Vegetable Soup, **74–75**

Chickpea, Tomato, and Pasta Soup, **130–131**

Coco Melon Lime Cooler, **52**

Cranberry Lemonade, **104–105**

Creamy Orange and Carrot Smoothie, **110–111**

Easy Minestrone Soup, **132–133**

Easy Slow Cooker Pumpkin Pie Rice Pudding, **164–165**

Egg and Avocado Breakfast Burritos, **56–57**

Fantastic Fudge Pops, **144–145**

Ginger Lime Energizer, **52**

Gingerade, **153**

Grapefruit Fizz, **106–107**

Italian Wedding Soup, **135**

Kiwi Pineapple Chia Smoothie, **154–155**

Lavender Lemonade Relaxer, **52**

Lean, Green, Broccoli Smoothie, **110–111**

Low Fiber

For digestion before competition and during recovery.

Index

About the **Authors**

MICHAEL KIRTSOS, MS, RD, CSSD, LDN, is Director of Nutritional Services/Clinical Nutrition Manager for HealthSouth Acute Rehab Hospital. He also is an adjunct professor of sports nutrition at Salisbury University and has been a board member for the Maryland Dietetic Association. Michael is board certified in sports dietetics by the Academy of Nutrition and Dietetics. He holds a Master's degree in applied health physiology/exercise physiology, with a concentration in strength and conditioning.

JOSEPH EWING, RD, LDN, is a clinical dietitian with Genesis Healthcare, a freelance dietitian, and a personal chef. He is the author of four cookbooks, among them *Idiot's Guides®: The Chia Seed Diet.* He holds degrees in culinary nutrition and culinary arts from Johnson and Wales University and completed a dietetic internship program at the University of Maryland.

Acknowledgments

Special thanks to chef and photographer Tom Hirschfeld (bonafidefarm food.com), for his exquisite photography. Many thanks also to Anthony Armstrong, executive chef at Nicolina's and director of food and beverage for the Indianapolis Wyndham West, for help in preparing the dishes for the photos. Thanks to Tara Deal Rochford, ACE Certified Personal Trainer and food blogger at Treble in the Kitchen (trebleinthe kitchen.com), for her thorough testing of each recipe. And thanks to Nigel Wright of XAB Design (xabdesign.com), for his masterful art direction and prop styling. We also would like to thank our families and friends for their constant encouragement and support.

PICTURE CREDITS

Dorling Kindersley would like to thank the following for their kind permission to reproduce their photographs:

8-9 istock©pixitive, istock©4x6. 10 Dave King, Roger Dixon. 11 Dave King, Ian O'Leary. 12 Ian O'Leary. 15 Zygote Media Group. 16 William Reavell. 17 Zygote Media Group. 24-25 Ian O'Leary. 28 William Reavell. 29 Dave King. 33 Roger Dixon, Roger Phillips. 36 Dave King, Peter Anderson, William Reavell, Roger Norum, Howard Shooter. 37 Steve Gorton, Julio Rochon, Will Heap, Getty Images/Sabine Scheckel/Photodisc, Tony Briscoe. 40 Dave King. 41 Howard Shooter, Philip Wilkins. 50-51 istock©pixitive, istock©4x6. 102-103 istock©pixitive, istock©4x6. 148-149 istock©pixitive, istock©4x6. 215 Dave King, Clive Bozzard-Hill. 217 Fotolia: Picsfive.

All other images Tom Hirschfeld.